A GIFT FOR:

....

FROM:

....

God's Shelter for Your Storm

© 2011 by Sheila Walsh

Published in Nashville, Tennessee by Thomas Nelson®. Thomas Nelson is a trademark of Thomas Nelson, Inc.

Published in association with the literary agency of Alive Communications, Inc., 7680 Goddard St., Suite 200, Colorado Springs, CO 80920

This edition published in 2011 by Hallmark Gift Books, a division of Hallmark Cards, Inc., Kansas City, MO 64141 Visit us on the Web at Hallmark.com.

Scripture quotations are taken from HOLY BIBLE: NEW INTERNATIONAL VERSION®. © 1993, 1978, 1984 by International Bible Society. Used by permission of Zondervan Publishing House. All rights reserved.

ISBN: 978-1-59530-439-1
BOK4137

Printed and bound in China

SHEILA WALSH

God's Shelter

FOR YOUR STORM

Table of Contents

Introduction

Between a Rock and a Hard Place

THE STORMS OF LIFE ARE NOT DISCRIMINATING. We all experience them no matter our age or status. Any one of us at any time can find ourselves surprised by joy one minute and overwhelmed by grief the next. We don't get that job we had counted on. The man we love suddenly decides he doesn't love us back. The test results come back positive. Our children make bad choices and take paths we never would have chosen for them. Someone we love dies.

When these storms come, it's our human nature to become anxious, even fearful, as we step into the unknown of what lies ahead. We get tired and confused and sometimes even lose our way as the weight of life presses down. But we're told in God's Word that we shouldn't be surprised when we encounter these tough times. After all, Jesus Himself experienced them; why should we expect an easier path? Jesus promised that although we would face tribulation, to take heart (John 16:33). For He has overcome.

And that was only *one* of His promises to us. When life throws us curves, when people disappoint us, when circumstances make us question our faith, we have His promises of hope to hold on to in the tough times. When we open God's Word, we are greeted with truths like these: God is faithful, He loves you, He is all power-ful, nothing is impossible for Him, He is always good, and He will never let you go. What a gift!

Through His written Word as well as in conver-sations with fellow believers, in our prayer time and our times of worship, we can hear God saying, *I am with you, and I always will be. I know life is hard. So I provide relationships that refresh and sustain, truths that enable you to persevere and keep hoping, and My Spirit to guide and strengthen you. And I Myself am always here for you.*

When I began to pray about this book, one spe-cific objective served as a plumb line for my writing: *What are the promises of God the Father and Jesus, His Son, that we can stake our lives on?* The Bible contains many more promises than those in this book. In fact, more than three thousand promises take us from the first page of Genesis to the last words of Revelation. But I chose ten promises that serve as foundation stones in a shelter that can help us weather the worst storms.

As I worked through the material and read and reread the chapters, I began to see a picture emerge that initially I had not even considered. As the mist of deadlines and busyness began to clear, I saw something that was breathtakingly beautiful to me. I saw not only that all God's promises of shelter are fulfilled in Christ, but that He *is* our Shelter. He *is* the cleft in the rock. Christ's promise to us is not that He will give us shelter but that He will *be* our Shelter.

When we know God's promises to us and trust that Christ will indeed be our Shelter, we can know that we are loved, safe and protected, and spared despite the tough circumstances of life. The writer of Psalm 121 knew that feeling of security and praised God for that blessing:

I lift up my eyes to the hills—

>*where does my help come from?*

My help comes from the LORD,

>*the Maker of heaven and earth.*

He will not let your foot slip—

>*he who watches over you will not slumber;*

indeed, he who watches over Israel will neither

>*slumber nor sleep.*

The LORD watches over you

>*the LORD is your shade at your right hand;*

the sun will not harm you by day,

>*nor the moon by night.*

The LORD will keep you from all harm—

>*he will watch over your life;*

the LORD will watch over your coming and going

>*both now and forevermore.*

This so-called Song of Ascents—one of fifteen psalms the faithful Jews sang as they climbed the road on their pilgrimage to Jerusalem to worship God—may become your own song of ascent. By God's grace, you will come to celebrate the shelter He promises and provides. And by His grace, you can—like the psalmist—learn to sense the Lord's constant presence with you and to be aware of His help, His watchful eye on your comings and goings, and His keeping you from harm. And when you're in the storm and under pressure, when you feel as if you're between a rock and a hard place, God will take you—as He has faithfully taken me again and again—to a place of rest, comfort, and hope.

In His love,

Sheila

Promises, Promises

Anchors in Life's Storms

FOR NO MATTER HOW MANY
PROMISES GOD HAS MADE,
THEY ARE "YES" IN CHRIST.
AND SO THROUGH HIM THE
"AMEN" IS SPOKEN BY US TO
THE GLORY OF GOD.

—2 CORINTHIANS 1:20

PINKIE PROMISE!... *Cross my heart and hope to die!* . . . We grow up on promises. We start making promises when we're young, and our friends make promises to us. With those promises comes a sense of security—and who doesn't want that, whatever the age!

I was past the pinkie-promise stage when I first started learning about God's promises in Scripture. But my desire to do an in-depth study of these promises actually began with a letter—an actual delivered-to-my-mailbox letter, which is rare these days. I picked up the hand-addressed envelope and began to read.

I had never met the woman who wrote to me, but apparently she had heard me speak at an event and sensed a connection with me. She wrote about some of the struggles she had been through in the past few years. These were not small things: illness,

financial hardship, and the breakup of her marriage. Amid her overview of these hardships, one line arrested my attention because of its profound simplicity:

"I would not have made it this far without the promises of God."

I read her letter again. I heard enormous pain, but at the same time I heard an unshakable faith in God. To some, the scales in this woman's life might seem imbalanced: the tangible hardships of her life had left her body, heart, and soul stripped bare. Yet her confidence in her God was compelling—beautifully and almost heartbreakingly compelling. Her words didn't read like wishful thinking but as a proclamation she had lived out in an *I know that I know*, tear-bathed way.

From the darkened caves of countless hearts, I have heard the same primal cry, the same questions over and again:

Has God forgotten me?
Does my life matter?
Is there a plan somewhere in all of this mess?
How am I going to make it?
How do I know God cares about my family?
Will I die alone?
Why won't God heal my depression?
Why hasn't God restored my marriage?
How do I know that God even heard my prayer?

We have pain that runs so deep that its presence, a reminder of the past, invades our lives over and over again. The aching hurts, failures, disappointments, and regrets keep us questioning: Do God's promises hold fast when life is falling apart around us? Can we trust Him to keep His promises? What exactly does He promise us anyway?

THE PROMISE ... FOR KEEPS

My husband, Barry, our son, Christian, and I loved having William—Barry's dad—living in our home for the last several months of his life. He was funny and sweet, and we were so glad that we could watch over him and simply enjoy him. But then one day we were discussing something at dinner. I don't even remember what it was now, but whatever I was saying, William disagreed with me and said so. We were all quiet for a moment. Then he pushed back his seat from the table and went upstairs to his room.

When he didn't come down after an hour, I decided to see if he was feeling okay. I knocked on his bedroom door, and William invited me in. "So do I leave now?"

I was stunned. "Of course not! Why would you ask that?"

"Well, I know you said I could stay forever." He paused. "But I broke the house rules. I wasn't kind to you."

I thought back to his comment at dinner, and I guess, to him, his leaving the table registered as unkindness toward me. "Pop, rules might give us some order, but love and grace make life worth living. You belong here. You are allowed to mess up just like any one of us. Besides, we threw away the sales receipt when we brought you home, Pop. We're keeping you!"

THE PROMISE OLDER THAN MOSES

Keeping is what we long for, and *keeping* is what God promises us. We hope, we wish, we pray for promises we can count on, come rain or shine, to shelter our hearts and our being, our dreams and our doings. We want these promises to be kept whether we mess up or when someone else does. We want to believe in our heart of hearts that God makes and keeps His promises to us, regardless of our faithfulness to Him.

And we are often totally unfaithful. Remember when the children of Israel melted down their jewelry, made a golden calf, and worshipped it? Moses was enraged, heartbroken, and devastated. God was devastated too—so shattered that He told Moses that maybe He should leave His people.

When Moses begged Him not to abandon His people, God's heart was moved: He was unable to leave those He loves or resist their cries. In the dust and rubble of the broken tablets on which He had first written the Ten Commandments, His Word remained true, and He would keep His promises.

God looked on Moses as he begged not only to stay in God's presence but to see all of God's glory. Acting on His infinite mercy, God commanded Moses to get two more tablets for another set of the Ten Commandments. Then He directed Moses to the cleft of Horeb, a cleft meant not only for protection from the storms but this time for the chance for Moses to see God's glory.

This cleft pointed to Christ, the ultimate Cleft, the Rock of Ages. In Christ, you can know protection from whatever storms are raging in your life, and you will see God's glory as He keeps His promises, sustains you, blesses you, and keeps you.

CHRIST IS THE CLEFT, THE KEEP

This is the shelter of all God's promises: *God not only keeps His promises, but He longs to keep us in them.*

Did you know that in those rock-and-stone castles of long ago, the very center tower was called the "keep"? It provided shelter, a place of habitation, an operating station from which defense, under siege, was centered. Usually a well was built at

He will take care of you, no matter how loudly your current situation is shouting otherwise.

the center of the keep so those sustained there could not only endure but thrive.

In God's kingdom, there is a keep too, and it is Christ. The apostle Paul put it this way: "No matter how many promises God has made, they are 'Yes' in Christ. . . . He anointed us, He set his seal of ownership on us" (2 Corinthians 1:20–22). God claimed us through Christ—He has made an eternity-long commitment to us that He cannot break. But we can be so unfaithful. Sometimes in our pain or panic, we forget His promises. Why would God want to keep us, and His promises to us, when we mess up so badly?

The Bible reminds us of a truth we too often forget, a truth that shines as clear as daylight. Why would God want to keep us and His promises to us? Because He cannot help Himself. The force of His righteousness and mercy are the unchanging foundation upon which His promises are built. God does not change. God's promises are as dependable as He is. Because they *are* Him.

GOD'S PROMISES ARE NOT LIKE OURS

Do you remember the Old Testament prophet named Balaam? Yes, the one whose donkey talked back to him (Numbers 22:22–35). Hear what even the heathen Balaam learned: "God is not man, that he should lie, nor a son of man, that he should change his mind" (23:19). Balaam could not help but recognize what is true: God cannot lie. And this from a man who, we're told, had no love for God or any desire to change his own self-serving ways. I love the fact that we are given those words not from a devout follower of our Father but rather from an outsider who recognized the truth of who God is and that, without exception, He does what He says He will do. When God speaks, He cannot lie. He means what He says, and He says what He means.

When God makes us a promise, He can never break it. If a heathen prophet can live by this understanding, how much more can we whom God has restored? Yet we have a lifetime of experiencing pain and heartache on one side of the scales and a simple, profound promise on the other: God cannot lie. Our human experience does not sync up with that heavenly truth. We have to separate promises that may never be kept from God's promises that will never be broken. I wonder if we have a hard time believing this, a hard time resting in God's promises, because we have been lied to so many times and because so many earthly promises are broken.

We are told: If you follow this diet, you will lose twenty pounds in two days. If you use this face cream, you will look twenty years younger in two weeks. If you use this shampoo, your hair will be full and flowing as it sparkles and shimmers in the breeze. Culture has driven us to think that promises are all about personal fulfillment, but God's promises are not about us—they are about Him and our being saved by Him. God's promises are an expression of His holiness. Furthermore, God keeps us not only to give us a future, but also to reflect His

glory. He keeps His promises to us because He cannot help Himself. He cannot lie, and He is full of love for His creation.

To put this truth in more personal terms, God cannot lie to you, and He is full of love for you. You are His beloved child.

FROM THE CLEFT BACK TO THE GARDEN

From the very beginning, God made a promise and had a plan. You can trace His promises back to the garden of Eden. Cursing the serpent, God said, "I will put enmity between you and the woman, and between your offspring and hers; he will crush your head, and you will strike his heel" (Genesis 3:15). God promised that the seed of Adam and Eve—Jesus Christ—would crush Satan's head and destroy him for eternity. Satan would bruise Christ's heel, meaning He would experience pain and suffering. Here God promised that there is a limit to the time that the enemy will have free reign on this earth.

When life is hard, we need to remember that we are travelers in this world, headed back to our true home with God, and that we come upon detours in our journey. Each detour takes us from the garden to a cross on a hill, where Christ Himself paid the ultimate sacrifice so that we can be free. Even as Christ was placed in a grave carved into a cleft of rock, He went there as a fulfillment of God's promise that death would be swallowed up in victory, for no grave could hold Him.

In fact, during the worst storms of our lives, God invites us to find our safe hiding place in Him. Our faithlessness does nothing to diminish God's faithfulness. We can therefore stake our lives on whatever God says. And Christ came to show us who our Father is. In Christ all the promises of God are fulfilled, for no matter how many promises God has made, they are "yes" in Him (2 Corinthians 1:20).

Normally we doubt whether a promise maker will be a promise keeper. But the witness of the substitutionary atonement of Jesus is that God has kept His most difficult promise to fulfill.

The Father is truly the only Promise Maker who is in earnest a Promise Keeper.

A promise from God is a promise kept.

There are His promises and His unbreakable commitment to keep them.

There is Christ. There is yes.

I Believe;
Help My Unbelief

Provision

My God will meet all
your needs according to
his glorious riches in
Christ Jesus.

—Philippians 4:19

CHRISTIAN WAS ABOUT TO TURN four, and his father and I were in full birthday-party-planning mode. How do you show a lifetime of love in a moment, in a day? Would Crackles the clown be the ticket? Or a jumpy-inflatable-castle thing? Jungle Jim from the zoo? Pony rides? Or llama rides? A face painter?

Well, long story short, all six of these birthday-party options showed up at our house, all at the same time—and as they filed out of our home that day, the children declared it the best party they had ever attended. The mothers did not look so thrilled. "What are we supposed to do now for our parties?" one asked. "Book the space shuttle?"

What had happened? Needing to know, I asked Barry. "Well," Barry said, still looking a little shell-shocked, "I asked them all to hold the date until I decided which one I wanted, and I forgot to get back to the others when I made my decision."

We looked at each other and fell on the floor laughing.

"Well, none of the moms are speaking to me," I said, "but Christian sure had a great party!"

THE PROMISE TO PROVIDE

On Christian's fourth birthday, my little family had way too much to offer, but that hasn't always been the case. There have been times when we feared we wouldn't have enough—enough money, time, energy.

Haven't we all been in that place of worry, fret, and fear when the needed provisions aren't at hand and don't seem to be coming? Maybe you're there right now. You are drowning in a sea of bills and feeling overwhelmed by everything that has to be taken care of and your awareness that there are not enough resources to meet the needs. The demands of life can seem crushing when you look at what you have and compare it to what you need. You can be left wondering, *Is God listening? Does He see? Will He fix things?*

But God is faithful; He will not disappoint. His provision for you will be in keeping with the wealth of His mercy as demonstrated in Jesus Christ. He takes care of His own. He will take care of you, no matter how loudly your current situation is shouting otherwise.

The unfailing promise is that God knows our needs, and as His track record shows, He will provide abundantly beyond what we can imagine. Yet the need to take care of ourselves is so deep within us. And when we can't, or when some great need outstrips our ability to handle it, the fear and desperation that set in can be brutal.

It's a feeling Jesus was familiar with.

JESUS KNOWS YOUR NEEDS

Try to put yourself in the position of Jesus' twelve disciples. Remember His marching orders when He sent them out on their first missions trip (Mark 6:7–12)? "Go out with a buddy."

So far, so good. "Take very little. No money or food. Just a staff to ward off wild animals." *What?!?* "Accept the first invitation to stay the night—and don't try to upgrade the accommodations during your visit." *What is Jesus expecting? Are we supposed to beg our way through the villages?* And then came Christ's command to cast out demons and heal the sick! It was one thing to watch Jesus conduct remarkable miracles, but quite another to be commissioned to do the same.

The experience must have been amazing as the disciples saw God use them to do the very things they had watched Jesus do: heal the sick, cast out demons, call many people to repentance. What a change from their previous jobs, from pulling fish out of the sea, collecting taxes, and guarding sheep. What an exciting moment when they all rejoined Jesus and reported on their missionary experiences. Jesus must have been deeply moved by His friends' stories and excited about their experiences, but we know He was wrestling with grief, too. His heart was broken over the news just received that John the Baptist had been beheaded by Herod Antipas. The disciples must have been distraught, too. John had given his life to prepare the way for Jesus—and his life ended in a barbaric way before a drunken crowd. Where had God been? What about His promise to provide protection and care?

PROVISION IS NOT PERFECTION

Upon hearing the news of John's death, Jesus' heart was heavy. So were His disciples' hearts. Mark 6:32 tells us simply, "So [Jesus and His disciples] went away by themselves in a boat to a solitary place." There are times when words don't help, when friends can't touch our grief. Our deepest need is simply to pull away with Christ.

Jesus understands your fear and fatigue, your disappointment and discouragement. Whatever you are facing, Jesus understands. He knows that heartbreak from worry and distress over provision, protection, and care can eat away at your peace, your hope. He understands the pain that comes when God doesn't seem to be keeping His end of the bargain. He understands that pain can be extreme (you lose a friend; a loved one dies) or more daily (you have to keep working with the office partner who feels compelled to criticize your every move). He also understands when external demands outweigh the internal strength required to simply stay afloat. Like when an unexpected doctor's visit leaves you with a bill bigger than your next six months' income.

Each of us can wear ourselves out stewing over how God will provide for us. But when we come to the end of ourselves, Jesus, our Cleft in the rock, calls: *Come away with Me. Find a quiet place with Me. Rest here with Me.* Just as Jesus in His times of distress sought time with His Father, we can seek shelter in Him when demands on our bodies, minds, and spirits threaten to undo us. God already has a plan to keep His promise and provide.

THE PROMISE OF WHAT'S POSSIBLE

Jesus sends us out to stand on God's promises and then invites us to retreat with Him when we're discouraged—but then to go back out again. When He does this, will we believe that He will do what He promises to do? Do we understand that, when it comes to provision, we can do nothing on our own anyway? That only in Jesus' name and only by resting in

Jesus can supply more than you will ever need.

Him, our Shelter, do we have something to stand upon and that, in that place, anything is possible?

I've had those moments. So often I am overwhelmed by what I don't have instead of by what Christ has given me.

The disciples were overwhelmed by what they didn't have when Jesus, after teaching the crowd until dinnertime, suggested that they see what kind of food they had available out in the middle of nowhere. And soon after they shared their concern, Jesus proceeded to feed the five thousand. It's the only miracle, in addition to the Resurrection, that appears in all four Gospels. What the disciples learned—and what I am learning, too—is that how far the provisions will go is not the issue. The issue is whose hands those provisions are in.

JESUS ALWAYS GIVES MORE

I wonder how many times the disciples had to come back to Jesus to get more as they distributed the food to such a huge crowd. Think about it. There were just twelve of them and perhaps ten thousand people. So they come back over and over and over again to refill their baskets, and each time I imagine the message going a little deeper: *Jesus can supply more than you will ever need. Jesus can supply more than you will ever need. Jesus can supply more than you will ever need.*

Jesus didn't simply provide enough for everyone, but much more than enough. He didn't choose a master chef or big food distributor, but a poor boy and his little lunch. God, after all, has Jesus looking out not only for our immediate needs, but for our ultimate needs, too: our knowledge that in Christ we have belonging and purpose, value and worth.

After all the crowd was fed, their immediate needs met, Jesus once again retreated. Even the Son needs His Father for rest and restoration, for God's providence, glory, and shelter.

And so Jesus, exhausted, went into the mountains to be

alone with God. The disciples, meanwhile, returned to the boat and set sail for Capernaum. They were tired from all they had been through: wonders and trials on the road in ministry, heartbreak and fear over the murder of their friend John the Baptist, stress from the crowds following them, amazement at another miracle by Jesus, physical exhaustion from the food distribution and crowd control of thousands of people.

Of course, a storm arose. Isn't that just how life goes? You are taxed and pressed by demands, you are worried and concerned about how all is going to work out, and just when an opportunity for rest comes, so does another storm.

So the wind was blowing, waves were crashing, and the disciples were straining and striving to stay afloat. And then they spotted a figure approaching them—a man walking on the water. They were terrified. Their hearts, like their little boat, were battered and sinking deep into confusion.

Then Jesus identified Himself: "It is I; don't be afraid" (John 6:20).

Eagerly, the disciples pulled Him into the boat, and according to John 6:21, they were immediately at the land to which they were going. Not only had Jesus gotten them through the storm, but He'd gone further for the disciples and delivered them to their destination.

In the feeding of the five thousand, the miraculous bread— more bountiful than anyone could ever eat—is a symbol of Jesus Himself, the divine sustenance that comes from nothing yet fulfills our every need . . . and then some! Christ's answer to the crowd that day is His answer to us: "I am the bread of life. He who comes to me will never go hungry, and he who believes in me will never be thirsty" (John 6:35).

Jesus told them, as He tells us: *I am everything you need. I am everything you need. I am everything you need.* Jesus doesn't simply supply our daily bread. He *is* our daily bread.

A PROMISE FOR ALL TIME

There is no need we have that God is not able and willing to meet. God does not need our money or our time or our resources, but He invites us into the divine adventure of partnering with Him to see what only He can do. In His grace, He loves to work through us. We can spend the rest of our lives looking at what we do not have, or we can bring everything we have and are to Him and watch miracles take place.

"My God will meet all your needs according to his glorious riches in Christ Jesus" (Philippians 4:19). We see in this promise that our kingdom work on earth reflects heaven: we see a need and meet it, and heaven sees all our needs and meets those. The apostle Paul commended the church in Philippi for the way they had poured out their resources to help him, and he expressed his confidence that God who knows their needs would more than meet them. This is a glorious promise! We give out of the little we have, and God in His grace and glory gives out of His limitless supply.

The miracle on the mountainside says, *Don't be consumed by what you don't have. Just bring what you do have to Jesus, and watch Him do what only He can do. And my God will meet all your needs.*

No matter what you are facing right now, Jesus says to you, *I am enough. I am enough. I am more than enough.*

"I am the bread of life.
He who comes to me will
never go hungry, and he
who believes in me will
never be thirsty."

JOHN 6:35

When Christ Speaks to the
Storms, They Obey

Peace

....

"Peace I leave with you;

my peace I give you."

—John 14:27

....

I MET HIM IN LONDON'S St. James's Park one spring day. He wore an old coat, even though it was a warm day, and it was tied at the waist by a piece of rope. On his feet were two plastic shopping bags. He was homeless.

When I asked him about his life, he looked at me with the saddest eyes I had ever seen and told me his story. At one time he had been a physician on Harley Street, a center known around the world for its medical excellence. Through a series of poor choices and an addiction to alcohol and prescription medicine, this gentle man in a coat frayed at the edges had lost his marriage and family, his medical license and career. He went from being a man who earned a huge salary and the respect of his peers to someone people avoided.

Then he said something I have never forgotten. He said that he was walking along Oxford Street one day when he passed a store that had mirrored doors. Out of the corner of his eye, he glimpsed something that caused him to take a second look.

"I saw an old man in a dirty shirt and unkempt hair," he said, "and as my distaste for him rose, I realized that it was me. This is what I had become."

THE PROMISE OF PEACE

My new friend in the park had become unrecognizable even to himself. Isolated and avoided, he lived in a place of unrest, loneliness, and self-loathing.

Do you know a place like this? Have you, too, found yourself tormented by life, in turmoil over the self-hatred you feel, and longing for peace, the kind of perfect peace that only Christ promises and can deliver? What does it look like, this peace that Jesus promised when He said, "Peace I leave with you; my peace I give you" (John 14:27)?

One man in the Bible, known as the Gadarene demoniac, lived in a place of unrest just as my friend in the park did. He, too, had become what he loathed, a man unkempt and unclean, living in isolation and fear—just the place where God promises to meet us, to drive out the demons of vexation and worry, torment and unrest, loneliness and self-hatred, and to bring us peace.

BENEATH THIS THING I'VE BECOME

Scripture doesn't explain either the physical or mental process of demon possession or how this tormented man ended up in such a wretched condition. When we meet the Gadarene demoniac, he is out of control. The tombs that had become his home were most likely caves cut into the side of the hill that offered shelter when the wind, coming off the sea, cut like a knife. A tempest raged within this poor man, too. His demon possession had led to inhuman strength: he could rip apart the irons that shackled him as if they were paper chains.

Jesus' disciples were not at all happy about heading to the Gadarenes. Crossing a storm-tossed sea in a dinghy toward a land of demons and occult worship, inhabited by potentially thousands of unclean pigs and tombs to mark countless corpses—it was a Jew's nightmare.

And the crossing there was no pleasure cruise. They encountered stormy seas that night, and their boat began to sink (Mark 4:37). Yet as the waves crashed against the boat and filled it, Jesus remained fast asleep in the stern. When the panicked disciples awakened Jesus, He stood up and spoke peace to the waves. "Quiet!" He said. "Be still!" (v. 39). The sea immediately became perfectly calm. When Christ speaks to storms—whether outside or inside the human heart—they obey.

"FOR WE ARE MANY"

Have you, like this tormented demoniac, ever been totally without hope? Maybe you're there now, and as far as you can tell, God has forgotten you. Maybe your life feels like a wasteland. Perhaps some devastating choices—yours or others'—have led you to places you never thought you would go and alienated those who have loved you. The horizon is barren and bleak. Without hope, the human spirit begins to check out of life. . . .

When Jesus stepped off the boat, the demons cried out, "What do you want with me, Jesus, Son of the Most High God? Swear to God that you won't torture me!" (Mark 5:7).

Jesus is not into negotiations, and He commanded the demons to leave the man. When the demons did not immediately obey Jesus, He asked them for their name. They replied, "My name is Legion . . . for we are many" (v. 9). (A legion was the largest unit of the Roman army, consisting of six thousand men.) It was quite a scene as—at Christ's command—this vast hoard of demons left one poor, battered man and entered a herd of two thousand pigs that proceeded to run squealing down a cliff and into the sea.

IN JESUS' PRESENCE, TOTAL PEACE

If I were one of the disciples, I would have been reaching for the Advil at this point . . .

After all, the moment I stepped off the boat, a crazed, demon-possessed man rushed me, and within moments his internal tormenters were flinging pigs off a cliff! As crazy as this scene was, in the presence of Jesus was total peace. Jesus looked upon the man, fatigued to his very soul and lying prostrate in the dirt. But for the first time in a very long time, he was serene, quiet, at the feet of Christ.

And the now-at-peace man begged to follow Jesus. He knew what darkness felt like, and he knew what Christ had done. But Jesus said no. He left this man as perhaps the first convert among the Gentiles to tell his story (Mark 5:20).

I wonder, though, how the man felt as he watched Jesus walk away and return to the boat. A vast and violent host of hatred had battled within him—until Jesus Christ showed up. Then the evil spirits had to leave. We don't know how long the man of the tombs lived after his exorcism, but I am confident that he became a radical disciple. After all, if you have tasted hell, you cling to the Lord of heaven.

So in a twenty-four-hour period, the disciples saw that Christ has power over the storms that rage in the world as well as those that rage within the human spirit. They watched as Jesus spoke peace, first turning a stormy sea into placid waters and then freeing a man from his internal, demon-driven storm.

Is there a storm raging around you? Or is one raging within you, wreaking havoc on your soul? The shelter Christ offers you brings peace; that shelter *is* peace.

FROM OUR OWN TOMBS

Some of us feel the torment of unrest because we have personally known a man of the tombs. I have. He was my father . . .

My dad was thirty-four years old when a brain aneurysm robbed him of the ability to speak and paralyzed the left side of his body. This wonderful daddy, who loved me very much, became a man of the tombs through no choice of his own. The impact of the damage to his brain seemed to come in waves. One moment he would be in his right mind and the next confused and angry. When he was himself, he

The shelter Christ offers you brings peace; that shelter is peace.

would weep, understanding that at times he was a frightening stranger to his family and himself.

I understand now, as an adult, what I couldn't understand as a child: my dad was ill and had no control over his rage. Through the years, God has brought much healing to this wound in my heart. My enduring sadness, though, has always come from wondering what it was like to feel trapped inside a body that betrayed you daily. I was able to receive peace from the Lord, but what of my father? What peace had he been able to know? It was in 2008, when I returned to the place where my father took his last steps on this earth, that I believe God answered that question. My father did not die in a hospital bed but in a river behind the hospital. He had escaped that night, and the doctors were unable to determine whether he had slipped and fallen in or if he had seen this as a way out of the caves of his illness.

I had never wanted to walk that shoreline, but I found myself there that day. As I stood at the place of nightmares, I felt Christ say to me, *I was there that night. Your father went from this earth to My arms, and I carried him all the way home.*

I now understand why I have always been drawn to stories of brokenness. For many years I felt that I had failed my dad by not saving him and that saving someone else would possibly give me a measure of peace. I now know that only Christ can save, that only He can bring peace. I also know His promise that life here doesn't have to be characterized by unrest and torment. We have but to look for Him on the horizon, run to Him, and ask for His peace. He can bring it with just a word, with only a glance.

Jesus sees us in the tombs, and He longs to take us to a better place, to a place of peace.

ONLY

can save. . .
ONLY HE
can bring peace.

Confidence

God Is Either Sovereign, or He's Not

WE KNOW THAT IN ALL
THINGS GOD WORKS FOR
THE GOOD OF THOSE WHO
LOVE HIM, WHO HAVE BEEN
CALLED ACCORDING
TO HIS PURPOSE.

—ROMANS 8:28

HIS WIFE WAS IN the hospital with what they thought was a bad case of the flu. But while she was there, her husband learned from his doctor that he was HIV positive. In utter despair, he realized that not only did he have the disease, but he had probably passed it on to his wife. And he had to tell her. So he bought a gun and drove to the hospital with the intention of telling his wife, facing her reaction, and then finding a quiet place to kill himself. But God had other plans.

As this husband sat by his wife's bed with tears pouring down his face, afraid to look into her eyes, he told her his story, the secret life where he had acted out his homosexual desires, the part of his life he had hidden from her for so long. He waited for her words to cut his soul to ribbons, but instead she reached out and took his hand. He looked up and saw that tears were pouring down her cheeks, too. She said, "Do you realize that this is the first time in our marriage I feel there is no distance between us—just the truth?"

They were both HIV positive, yet God—as only He can—used the husband's terrible secret to bring them closer to His heart and to each other. At the worst moment of their lives, they were surprised by God's grace, and they took shelter in His promise that He can bring good out of life's greatest heartaches.

THE PROMISE OF PURPOSE

God's promise in Romans 8:28 reads, "We know that in all things God works for the good of those who love him, who have been called according to his purpose."

But how can God use even the worst circumstances in life for good, to bring us closer to Him? Do we really believe He will take the most unlikely events and the most painful moments of life for our good and His glory? The confident assertion of this Romans 8:28 promise is that God will use *all* things for good.

We who, by God's Spirit, have been adopted into His family can rest assured that God is at work in our lives for good. Based on this truth, Paul boldly assured us that everything will work out in God's way and in His time. The result should be our deepest confidence in the heart of God and His love for us. If we patiently wait, we will see the unfolding of this tapestry of experiences into the establishment of His purposes. Our confidence flows out of His steadfastness.

That road, however, can be a strange one.

HOPE FOR THE MOST UNLIKELY ONE

Jesus had many fascinating encounters with women in the Gospel accounts, but His meeting with a Samaritan woman at the end of a hot and exhausting day was one of the most powerful.

To the pure-blooded Jew, the Samaritans were to be despised and avoided at all costs, yet Scripture says Jesus "had to go through Samaria" (John 4:4)—and not just because that was the shortest route from Judea to Galilee. The Greek for *had to* means "divine necessity" or "command." Jesus *had to* take that road—there was a woman who needed to know that her life mattered. Even before the promise that "God causes all things to work together for good for those who have been called" was ever put down in words, Christ, the Promise, was about to make all things work together for the good of a very lost soul.

To better understand how radical Christ's interaction with this Samaritan woman was, consider that, at the time, many Jewish men began their day by thanking God that they were not a Gentile, a slave, or a woman—in that order. So Jesus' conversation with this woman was definitely a shocking encounter. But Christ saw beyond the cultural barrier to a broken life.

When Barry and I lived in Nashville in the late 1990s, I regularly visited the Humane Society. One cat named Max especially drew my attention. One cold night, Max had crawled under the hood of a car and onto the still-warm engine. When the owner of the car started the engine the next morning, he heard a loud cry as Max's back received an awful wound, about six inches long. The owner of the car brought Max to the shelter, and the vet did what he could, but Max was a sorry sight. He had no fur left on his back, and the fur on the rest of his body had been cut very short to remove the oil that had matted there and was now growing back at bizarre angles left and right.

When I heard a Humane Society volunteer say, "I'm not sure how we'll ever get him adopted," I took Max home that day. He was one of the sweetest animals I have ever had the joy of loving. It seemed to me that his devotion came from someone seeing beyond his wounds to his wonderful heart.

Perhaps that is what is most striking about Christ's encounter with the Samaritan woman at the well: He saw beyond her culture, her gender, and even her choices. He saw a woman who was worth dying for and who would bind her heart to His, with all her heart, and she would never forget. She would see that the lonely path she had walked for so long was the one that brought her to the well that day. All the wrong choices and broken dreams had worked together to lead her to Christ, the Shelter.

GOOD HAPPENS

Before this encounter, however, Jesus was worn out, fatigued, sore, and exhausted. Yet His love compelled Him to keep walking when He wanted to sit down, to let the crowd touch Him when He wanted to be alone, and, here, to reach a woman who had made many poor choices and let her know that she was loved.

So Jesus sat down, His disciples having gone into town to buy some food. It was highly irregular for Jewish men to go into a Samaritan village to buy food—but Jesus sent them, so they went. He wanted to encounter this woman alone. And not only is that a remarkable thing, but add this: Jesus spoke first.

Jesus said to her, "Will you give me a drink?" (John 4:7).

The woman was surprised to be addressed by a man, especially a man who was obviously a Jew. Then Jesus, never known for small talk, got right to the heart of the matter and her need: "If you knew the gift of God, and who it is that asks you for a drink, you would have asked him and he would have given you living water" (v. 10).

I wonder how Jesus' words impacted this woman. She

was probably living with a drought-stricken soul and spirit, struggling to get from one day to the next, when an unlikely stranger with a compelling gaze offered her living water. And this woman wanted to know exactly how Jesus would provide this liquid refreshment when He didn't even have a bucket.

Jesus got right to the heart of her need and her story. He told her what every one of us who has ever struggled in this life before finding a relationship with Christ knows: nothing in this world will satisfy us for long. Even the things that we believe will make us happy only do so for a moment.

The Samaritan woman knew that to be true, and Jesus was about to present her with an opportunity to come clean.

He asked her to go home and bring her husband back to the well. Interesting request.

MOMENT OF TRUTH

This was the Samaritan woman's moment of truth. As she looked into the eyes of Jesus, I believe she decided that, whatever the consequences, she could not lie to Him, so she told Him half of the truth: "I have no husband" (John 4:17).

Knowing that she had risked a little of herself, Jesus told her that He knew the whole truth. One of the most redeeming graces of Christ is that He tells us the whole truth about ourselves without shaming us. Christ revealed that not only did He know that was true, but He knew who she was with now and how many times she had been married before.

Do you see the compelling confidence this promise offers? Christ knows all that is true about our story, the parts we own and the parts we would delete, and He invites us to bring them all into the spotlight of His grace.

This woman had finally been exposed, but in the redemptive love and grace of Jesus. Clearly, God uses even the very acts that Satan would use to destroy us to help us find our way home to His heart.

*Christ*

KNOWS ALL THAT IS TRUE
ABOUT OUR STORY,

*the parts we own and
the parts we would delete,*

and He invites us to bri

...em all into the spotlight of his grace.

GOOD FOR HER AND GOOD THROUGH HER

What is amazing from this account is how we are shown that God not only works all things for our own good, but He also redeems our lives and works through us as well. In this case, the Samaritan woman became an evangelist to her hometown of Sychar!

If we're honest with ourselves, we are all, to some degree, this Samaritan woman. Until we come face-to-face with Christ, we are buried in sin and sinfulness. But He can and does deliver us out of the oppressive story we find ourselves lost in. With the water of life, He washes us, refreshes us, and sends us out with the privilege of sharing with others what we have received. This was the Samaritan woman's experience as well . . . because of Christ's commitment to graft her life into the goodness of who He is and all He intended for her.

RESTING IN THE CONFIDENT ASSURANCE THAT GOD IS IN CONTROL

This brand-new believer was given the gift of seeing that, in God's hands, even the worst moments of her life could bring good to herself and to those around her. Jesus didn't seek out the most reputable person in the village to share Himself with. He sought out a Samaritan woman with a bad reputation—the lowest of the low in that culture—to show that, in God's hands, even the things that have broken us can be used by Him to make us whole again. There are no accidents in God's kingdom.

I could sit with that one truth for some time. Think about your life through that window: *there is no accident*. How does that feel to you? It might be difficult to come to terms with if there have been many moments in your life that have felt cruel or out of control. How can breast cancer or sick children or any other tragedy possibly work for good? This is a mystery worth wrestling with, because once we grasp the radical truth contained in this

Our calling is to be conformed, to be made like Christ.

promise of purpose, it will change how we view every moment of our lives.

Specifically, if we are able by God's grace to receive the truth that every single thing in our lives will work together for good, it will transform not only how we embrace our circumstances but ultimately the purpose of our lives, which is to become more like Christ (Romans 8:29). Our calling is to be conformed, to be made like Christ. In this Christlikeness is our confidence.

I don't pretend to understand everything you have been through, but I do know that you are loved and cared for by a Master Refiner who never takes His eyes off you.

ALL THINGS WORK TOGETHER FOR GOOD?

You may marvel, as I have, at how God worked things for good in the Samaritan woman's case. But you may be asking this very legitimate question: *All things, everything, work together for the good?*

You've probably not heard of Samuel Logan Brengle, a leader in the early Salvation Army movement whose writings on holiness are spiritual classics. Samuel never intended to be a writer, but he felt God calling him to the pastoral ministry. A compelling speaker, Samuel wanted to be not only a good preacher but the best. But God had other plans.

One night, as Samuel returned home from a Salvation Army meeting he had conducted in Boston, a drunken man who had been ejected from the meeting for disruption threw a large paving brick at Samuel's head. For some time, Samuel hovered between life and death because of the blow. It took him a full eighteen months to recover. During those eighteen months he began to write. Initially he wrote articles, but they were so powerful that they were gathered together and published as the book *Helps to Holiness*. Sometime later, his wife presented him with the very brick that had injured him.

On it she had written: "As for you, ye thought evil against me; but God meant it unto good, to save much people alive."[1]

THIS DOESN'T FEEL GOOD

Many things in life do not feel as if they are working together for good at all. We live in a fallen world, a broken planet. I no longer expect anything to be the way it should be, but I take great comfort, courage, and strength from the promise that in the midst of the brokenness, the Holy Spirit intercedes for us. I would expect that the depth of His groaning corresponds to the depth of our pain. There are times in life when words just do not come. You may find yourself in a place that is darker than you ever imagined, and you want to cry out, "How can this work out for good?"

I want you to know that you have a Prayer Partner in heaven, pleading for you before the throne of grace and mercy. When you don't even know what to pray, the Holy Spirit does.

He is God, which means He is all-powerful and all-knowing. You are not alone.

Imagine asking the Samaritan woman if she would make the same choices if she had her life to live over again. She might say something like this: "My sin and my brokenness prompted many bad choices, and my bad choices led to more bad choices. But every poor choice took me one day closer to that day when I came face-to-face with Christ. For that reason alone, I would not change a moment."

As you reflect on your life, I pray that you can say with absolute confidence that, although there have been many turns in the road, God has used every bend to bring you under the shelter of His loving arms.

Love

*Jesus' Love Heals,
Transforms, and Gives Life*

I AM CONVINCED THAT NEITHER
DEATH NOR LIFE, NEITHER ANGELS
NOR DEMONS, NEITHER THE PRESENT
NOR THE FUTURE, NOR ANY POWERS,
NEITHER HEIGHT NOR DEPTH, NOR
ANYTHING ELSE IN ALL CREATION,
WILL BE ABLE TO SEPARATE US FROM
THE LOVE OF GOD THAT IS IN CHRIST
JESUS OUR LORD.

—ROMANS 8:38–39

RELENTLESS LOVE, characterized by His unwavering pursuit and His unshakable devotion—that is what God promised us in Romans 8:38. In fact, God pursued us to the point of becoming a human being. What an unspeakable gift that the almighty God would come to us in Christ, as a helpless babe, and eventually hang on a cross to show us His love. Jesus poured out His life for us so that, now and for all eternity, nothing can separate us from God's love. Nothing. Not time nor circumstances nor space. God loves us for keeps and tells us: *I love you outrageously and you belong to Me—forever*. What a comfort that declaration is for every heart wound you experience, every moment you feel castaway, unloved, and unwanted. What peace and joy that promise brings to a person who has been rejected, shunned. A promise like that could make the lonely, despairing soul dare to

reach out again. A promise like that shatters walls that isolate and floods a life with love enough to share.

LOOKING FOR LOVE

For twelve years, a woman, unnamed in the Gospels, knew what it was to be isolated. Suffering from and shamed by a medical condition that caused her to hemorrhage, she was deemed unclean by her Jewish culture, avoided, and ostracized. For twelve years, this woman had no community, no love, not even a kind touch. When Jesus came to town, she needed a miracle—as did Jairus, an important ruler of the synagogue in Capernaum. His daughter was critically ill.

Jairus begged Jesus to come and touch his daughter so that she would be healed. As He made His way through the crowd to Jairus's house, Jesus suddenly stopped. He had felt power leave Him; someone had touched Him with a touch of great faith. That someone was the woman with the issue of blood . . . who had long known pain in both body and soul. Imagine how desperate she felt, how shattered, isolated, unloved, and in complete despair.

Have you ever felt like that?

Yet she had not given up hope that, at a divinely appointed moment, love would be within arm's reach.

LOVE MAKES YOU TAKE RISKS

Capernaum and all the villages around Galilee were abuzz with news about Jesus. Everywhere He went, He was healing people and filling them with a new sense of purpose and joy.

If only I touch His clothes, I will be healed, she thought (Mark 5:28). But there was such a large crowd around Jesus. *What can I do?*

This woman shouldn't even be there. She was unclean, untouchable. Anyone or anything who touched her would also be unclean, untouchable for at least seven days. Plus, she couldn't ask Jesus to help her before He went to the house of Capernaum's leading rabbi, whose twelve-year-old daughter was dying! This suffering woman was the antithesis of Jairus's daughter, who was loved, fought for, and treasured. No one fought for this woman. She had no champion.

Have you ever been there? Are you there right now? Perhaps you learned a long time ago that fairy tales are cruel in their promises because no one came to your rescue.

But the possibility of love—of transforming, healing love—was too great. The woman made a life-changing decision. No matter what this act would cost her, how could her situation be any worse? She had spent everything already anyway: her finances, her very self. She was a walking dead woman.

Her crossroads makes me think of one very low point in my own life. A friend had said to me, "When the pain of staying the same is greater than the pain of change, then you will change."

That simple but profound statement stuck with me and comes to mind now. At times, the familiar place where we are, even if it is painful, offers a degree of comfort. Have you ever been in a place where you knew God was calling you to step out and grasp hold of life, but taking that step was just too scary?

The hemorrhaging woman was in that very place. She faced not only the possibility of public humiliation, but also sanctioning by the crowd and, worse, by Jairus the rabbi and by Christ Himself. Regardless of the consequences, how could the woman not take the risk when a possibility for change was *right in front of her?*

ℕOT WORTH SAVING

This woman's struggle with her social standing and loneliness would be torture enough, but imagine the mental and emotional anguish inside her heart and mind. She had been wrestling with self-hatred for *twelve years.* You know these lies. We've all heard them before, especially at those moments when God calls to us to take a risk and love as He loves:

Who do you think you are?

You will never change!

There is no hope for you.

If people knew who you really are, no one would want you.

Why do you keep trying? Things will never change.

You are worthless!

One of the enemy's greatest strategies is to make us believe that we are not worth saving and not worth loving. He will torment us with his evil accusations and lies, but he has no control over whether we will believe anything he says. So even as things in this life press in on us like that crowd, threatening to distance us from God and His love, try to exercise the faith of the hemorrhaging woman. In those hard moments, when you're questioning God's love for you, reject Satan's lie. Granted, his lies are subtle at first, and they feed into how so many of us already feel about ourselves. So start today to replace every lie with God's Word, with one of His promises from Scripture. You can reach out and touch the hem of Jesus' robe. Jesus is the eternal place of promise, the place where your miracle can happen.

FROM DESPAIR TO DAUGHTER

This ill and isolated woman, broken physically as well as emotionally, may have walked up to thirty miles to get to Capernaum. As Jesus got near, she chose to believe there was hope, and with every ounce of strength left in her body, she pushed through the crowd and reached out to grab the hem

Jesus is the eternal place of promise, the place where your miracle can happen.

of Christ's garment. A touch was all she could muster. But a touch was all she needed. So she reached out and touched the hem of Jesus' robe. Immediately the hemorrhaging stopped. Just like that. The pain disappeared. She was clean. She was revived. Instead of her life's blood flowing out of her, new life and power coursed through her veins.

How easily this woman could have slipped back into the crowd, privately elated by the miracle, content in knowing she had received just what was needed. But Jesus gives what He *knows* we need, and He wanted this woman who had lived so long unloved, untouched, to receive not just healing for her illness, but a relationship with Him that would change everything. So Jesus asked, "Who touched my clothes?" (Mark 5:30).

TELL YOUR STORY

The disciples thought this was one of the most ridiculous questions Jesus had ever asked. With the crowd pushing against Him, what did Jesus mean, "Who touched my clothes?"

But Jesus had felt the power of God flow from Him. And He didn't ask the question because He didn't know the answer or because He wanted to be thanked or any other reason. He asked because He loved the woman. He wanted to give her so much more than she knew to ask for: she wanted to be healed in her body, but Jesus wanted her to be healed in her mind, spirit, and relationships, too.

If the hemorrhaging woman had crept silently away that day, would she have wondered if she had stolen a miracle?

And Jesus didn't point to her when she touched Him and say, "It was you, wasn't it?" He let her decide whether she would step out or not: "Then the woman, knowing what had happened to her, came and fell at his feet and, trembling with fear, told him the whole truth" (Mark 5:33).

THE WHOLE TRUTH

What an amazing gift Christ gave this woman! He gave her a place to tell Him all that was true about herself and, in that most vulnerable moment, a chance to be fully seen and fully loved.

Have you ever told Jesus the whole truth about yourself? Scary thought for some of us, yet the great irony is that He already knows all that is true about us, and He loves us anyway. If the woman had slipped away that day, her body would have been healed, but residual shame might have been a new and ongoing affliction.

This brave, broken, healed woman fell at Jesus' feet and told Him everything. We don't know what she said, but I imagine she told Him how her affliction started and what it had cost her. She told Him how alone she had been for so long. She told Him about the shame and the pain and the fear. Perhaps she hoped for mercy, but she got much more: "He said to her, 'Daughter, your faith has healed you'" (v. 34).

Such tender, inclusive words to someone who had been an outcast for so long! Everyone around Jesus that day heard Him

say this. He declared that her faith in Him had brought her healing and wholeness, and then He sent her off with a blessing: "Go in peace and be freed from your suffering" (v. 4).

WHAT ABOUT JAIRUS'S DAUGHTER?

As wonderful as this miracle of healing and restoration was, if I were Jairus, I might have been completely annoyed or even angry. His dying daughter was his concern. He was consumed with a sense of urgency. His heart was beating out of his chest. Every second that Jesus spent here, listening to this woman's story, was another second his daughter was closer to death. And then the word came: "Your daughter is dead" (v. 35). When Jesus heard the news, He turned to Jairus and said, "Don't be afraid; just believe" (v. 36).

Then, leaving the crowd and allowing only Peter, James, and John (James's brother) to accompany Him, Jesus went to Jairus's house. Picture the love and compassion in His eyes as He looked at the frenzied grief. He offered words to calm the grieving people, to give them peace. "Why all this commotion and wailing?" He said. "The child is not dead but asleep" (v. 39).

The people laughed at Jesus, but Jesus put out everyone from the house except Jairus and his wife and Peter, James, and John. He went to where the little girl was and took her by the hand. "Little girl, I say to you, get up!" (v. 41).

Straightaway the little girl got up and began to walk around.

WHAT KIND OF LOVE IS THIS?

I find it interesting that Jairus's daughter was *twelve* years old and that for twelve years the hemorrhaging woman had suffered. For twelve years, Jairus had loved his little girl. For every day of his daughter's life, the woman had been in pain. When his little girl learned to crawl, the woman was in pain. When his little girl took her first step, the woman was suffering. When his little girl was old enough to spend the night at her best friend's house, this woman was still crying out in the darkness.

These twelve years were no coincidence, illustrating so clearly two things about God and His promise to love us. First, your status in life makes no difference to God's love for you. Christ treats every person, whether child or aged, afflicted or physically whole, with a dignity that our world does not. He did not say to the woman, "I'd love to hear your story—after I take care of this important man's daughter." No, He took all the time she needed right there and then.

The second thing is a greater mystery. Jairus's little girl was allowed to struggle for only a short time before Christ healed her, but the hemorrhaging woman waited twelve years. There are some things on this earth that we will never understand.

What we do need to remember, though, is that pain is pain, whether it's a girl's or a woman's. Suffering is suffering, whether it hurts for a short time or for years. Loss is loss, whether it takes away something for a moment or a lifetime. And the love that heals all, transforms all, and gives life to all—that is the love that Jesus has for you.

So how long have you been bleeding? Very few of us will ever know the kind of physical loss of blood that this woman faced, but how long have you been bleeding from shame or a wound so deep that you believe it will never heal? I invite you to go to the feet of Christ and tell Him your whole story.

"Neither death nor life, neither angels nor demons, neither the present nor the future, nor any powers, neither height nor depth, nor anything else in all creation, will be able to separate us from the love of God that is in Christ Jesus our Lord" (Romans 8:38–39).

THE LOVE THAT
HEALS ALL,

transforms all,

AND GIVES LIFE TO ALL—
*that is the love
that Jesus has for you.*

Grace

It's Not Too Good to Be True

....

"MY GRACE IS SUFFICIENT
FOR YOU, FOR MY POWER IS
MADE PERFECT IN
WEAKNESS."

—2 CORINTHIANS 12:9

....

WHEN WE VISITED the funeral home after my mother-in-law, Eleanor, died, the last conversation I had with her played in my mind. . . .

"Sheila," she asked, "I know we have talked about this before, but do you really believe that God loves me as much as He loves you?"

"With all my heart I do," I said.

"I'm not so sure. Don't you think He must love some more than others? The good ones, the ones who give Him all their lives, the ones who don't make so many mistakes?"

"Mom, God's love for us is based on who He is, not on how we act," I said. Even as I said that, I thought of one of Eleanor's favorite expressions, "Straighten up and act right!"

"Mom, I know that for most of your life you have

believed that God's love is based on whether we make good choices or bad choices, but the cross makes it clear that no amount of good choices would ever be enough. You are loved just the same on the days when you feel you've done a good job as on the days when you know you've blown it."

"I know you believe that," she whispered. "It's just hard to hold on to."

THE PROMISE OF GRACE

Eleanor was right. It is hard to believe that God loves each of us equally, without measure or merit, and that His grace shelters us regardless of what we do or what we leave undone. I think it's so hard to believe because there is no other relationship on earth like it. Every other relationship we have is affected, to some extent, by how we behave and what we say.

If we abuse a friendship in any way, there are consequences. We become more distant and formal. At times, if our behavior is inappropriate enough, it will cost us that friend. The child who yells, screams, or refuses to listen to a parent has consequences. In marriage, a couple stands before God, family, and friends to vow love to one another until death parts them. Yet about half of all marriages end in divorce because of behavior and choices.[1] Every earthly relationship teaches us that love and acceptance are conditional.

That's why being loved forever based on nothing but someone else's ability to love us unconditionally is, as Eleanor said, "hard to hold on to." Doesn't each of us struggle to believe in such love, such grace? Doesn't each of us find that human love fails us, both intentionally and, as in death or tragic separations, unintentionally?

The only place we find unconditional, unwavering, unchanging love is in the heart of God our Father, expressed on this earth through Christ, His Son. That kind of divine love is grace.

When you hear the word *grace*, what comes to your mind?

I always heard *grace* defined as "unmerited favor." In the New Testament, *grace* also means "love," "goodwill," and "lovingkindness." The only requirement for receiving this grace, this unmerited favor, is a relationship with Jesus Christ. The grace of God, Paul wrote, is free, but we are never to regard it as a license to sin: "Shall we go on sinning so that grace may increase? By no means! We died to sin; how can we live in it any longer?" (Romans 6:1–2). So we have this gift that we can never earn or pay back, and we are called into relationship, where the closer we get to God's heart, the more like Him we become and the less we want to sin.

If this sounds complicated, know one thing that is crystal clear: God is always the initiator of this love and mercy—of the kind of strength that fills in our weaknesses, the kind of perfection that covers our flaws, and the kind of shelter that says, "I'm going to keep you and love you through all your failings." God pursues us and woos us to this place of grace, to His shelter.

When we mess up, God untangles the situation. When we are weak, He is strong. When we have no control over our imperfections, He offers His transforming touch and lovingly shows us the way He sees us. He patiently listens to our doubts and fears and then proclaims, *With all My heart, I'm telling you that*

there is nothing you can do to make Me love you more, and there is nothing
you can do to make Me love you less. You are loved and always will be loved,
and I am going to love you and forgive you to the very end.

THE EXTENT OF GRACE

Jesus emphasized this truth—God's pursuit of us—in story
after story. Nearly every illustration He gave reminds us of the
heart of God and the extent to which His grace will go to reach
us. In Jesus' parables about the lost sheep, the lost coin, and the
lost son, the theme is consistent: the lost cannot restore anything and, by God's grace, they do not need to (Luke 15).

In the story of the lost sheep, the shepherd who had one
hundred sheep left the ninety-nine to go and look for the one
that was lost. When he found it, rather than scold the sheep, he
put it on his shoulders and brought it home, inviting his neigh-
bors to rejoice with him that he had found this precious lamb.

In the story of the lost coin, a woman had ten coins. When
she realized that she had lost one, she lit a lamp and swept the
entire house until she found it. When she did, she invited all
those in her community to celebrate with her that what was

once missing was now found.

The most moving parable, that of the prodigal son, was perhaps, to the original hearers, also the most controversial. We often fail to realize how shocking it might have been to those who heard it from Jesus' lips. In part, maybe that's because we live in a culture bombarded by reality television and talk shows that survive on the heartache and poor choices of dysfunctional families. Even within Christian circles, it's not so unusual to hear of children who decide to reject their family's standards and head out to "find themselves." But the crowd Jesus spoke to heard that story as a tale of the greatest shame that could be brought on a family. The culture was very much a patriarchal society, and acting with respect and honor for the father was an unspoken mandate. Every element that Christ included in the parable added to its shock value:

- *A boy insulted his father by demanding his inheritance before his father was even dead. This would have deeply offended His listeners.*
- *To increase the insult, the son headed for the big city and, on one wild party after another, wasted the money his father had worked so hard to earn.*

❧ *When the son was finally destitute and scouring through the very food he was feeding the pigs (an unclean animal to the Jews, so to even be in their presence was an affront), he decided to return home and beg for a job on his father's estate. After what he had done, he should never show his face to his father again.*

As the crowd listened to Jesus tell the story, they must have anticipated hearing what kind of retribution the father would exact upon the son. But what they heard about was a father waiting expectantly with a heart full of mercy. *Mercy?* Unthinkable!

No one in the crowd that day would be prepared for the outcome of Jesus' story. Here He presented grace in its most stark and arresting form as the father ran to his son, welcomed him home with a hug and a kiss, dressed him in his best robe, and ordered that the fattened calf be killed and cooked for a celebration of his son's return.

A PARTY FOR SINNERS

As far as Jesus' audience was concerned, the prodigal son's father should have written off the boy. Instead, he watched for his boy every day, waiting, hoping that this might be the day he would come home. So many aspects of the story seemed outrageous: that this ungrateful and defiant son was worth everything to the father and that the father would *run* to greet this son when he did return home. It was truly undignified for the patriarch of a family to ever be seen running, and this father was running toward the son who had earlier defiled his dignity. There was no precedent for this kind of love and mercy, for this kind of grace.

The prodigal son had prepared a speech as he trudged the hot, weary miles home, but he never got a chance to get his confession and request for forgiveness out, for the father immediately began yelling instructions to the servants: "Bring the best robe in the house, put a ring on his finger as a sign that he is a beloved son, not a servant, and whatever animal we have been saving for a rainy day, kill it now, for grace is raining down!"

"This is outrageous!" the people listening to Jesus might have said.

And that was the whole point. The love God has for us is unprecedented, outrageous, and overwhelming, especially for

one man in the crowd—one of Jesus' disciples—who heard the story that day. Even though he had heard it, he had no idea how much he would need the truth of those words in the days to come.

Before we get to that, one more thought. Each time I have revisited this story through the years, I have found myself in unexpected places: I am the prodigal, and then I am the elder brother. Christ's masterful storytelling is like a mirror He holds up for us to see . . . if we will look. This mirror would be deeply offensive to the listening crowd that day, for in effect Christ was saying, "See yourself here. You are the central characters." And who—then or now—could disagree? Each of us in our own way has squandered what our Father has given us, perhaps not as blatantly as the younger son, but squandered it nonetheless. And don't you think every single one of us has felt a surge of self-righteous indignation when God's grace has welcomed back not just to the fold, but to a party for the person who offended us at a core level? Grace is offensive before it is liberating.

A PROMISE FOR PETER

Now back to the listening disciple . . . Little did Peter realize, as he listened to Jesus' teaching, how this story of failure and redemption would become his life song.

Peter began his life as a fisherman in Bethsaida, the same Galilean village that Nathaniel and Philip, two other disciples of Jesus, were from, and they all worked together. Peter's fishing business had obviously prospered, because by the time we meet him in the Gospels, he had moved to Capernaum, the leading city of Galilee, and gone into partnership with James and John, two other members of the Twelve. Clearly, Peter was a successful businessman who ran quite a fishing empire. But one day he met a Man who changed everything. When Jesus said, "Come, follow me," Peter did (Matthew 4:19).

What was it about Jesus that compelled Peter and Andrew to drop what they were doing and go with Him? I believe that they were called into mission with Jesus and felt it deeply. I'm sure that, at that stage, they had no idea what the day ahead would hold, never mind the coming weeks and months. But

Christ's MASTERFUL STORYTELLING *is like a mirror he holds u*

or us to see . . . if we will look.

they sensed the call of God and responded.

The role of disciple was hardly unknown in those days; it had a clear job description. People in those times enrolled not in a seminary but as students of an established rabbi. They would live with their master and learn by listening and asking questions. The greater goal of Jesus' followers was not just to learn from Christ but to become like Him.

A brief aside. It seems that the other eleven disciples looked to Peter as their leader. Consider that anytime the disciples are listed, Peter is always mentioned first. Even when the list is just Christ's three closest friends, Peter is always named before James and John. Whatever Peter's relationship was with his fellow disciples, he obviously had a special relationship with Christ. On one occasion early in their friendship, Jesus asked Peter to pull his boat out into deep water in the morning and put down his nets. Peter was a veteran fisherman who knew to fish at night in these waters, but because Jesus asked him to lower his nets, he did. When those nets began to fill to breaking point with fish, Peter asked Jesus to leave: "Go away from me, Lord; I am a sinful man!" (Luke 5:8).

Could it be that Peter was more aware of his own flawed humanity in the presence of Christ's holiness than we have supposed over the ages? Certainly Peter was struck by the Lord's perfection in comparison to his own imperfection. Remember, for example, the night the disciples spent in a boat, trying to get across the Sea of Galilee in a fierce storm.

It was evening, and Christ had just fed a crowd of five thousand men with five loaves of bread and two fish. Exhausted from that teaching time and heartbroken by the news of the execution of John the Baptist, Jesus sent the disciples on without Him while He headed to the hills to be alone with His Father. The disciples were having a hard time making any headway against the wind that was whipping the sea into a frenzy. At about three o'clock in the morning, they became aware of a figure walking toward them on the surface of the waves. Initially they were terrified, but Jesus called out and identified Himself.

Peter spoke up: "Lord, if it's you . . . tell me to come to you on the water" (Matthew 14:28). Jesus spoke that command, and Peter started walking toward Him on top of the water—

until the disciple took his eyes off his Master.

And I think Peter gets a bit of a bad rap here. We talk about his lack of faith, but he was the only one willing to get out of the boat at all. Peter had to face the harsh reality that our ways are not God's ways and that God's grace is made perfect in our weakness, not in what we perceive as our strength.

This truth is one of the greatest ironies of our faith: at the moment when we realize we have nothing to give Christ and we fall flat on our faces, we bring the gift He has been asking for all along. That gift is our hearts—not our ideas or skills or preferences. Just ourselves.

A FINAL MEAL

When the disciples gathered with Jesus to celebrate the Passover feast, Jesus addressed Peter with the warning that Satan wanted to test the disciples and the promise that Jesus Himself was praying that Peter would stand strong in his faith (Luke 22:31–34).

So why would Satan be allowed to mess with Christ's followers? And what is it about the process of pain and failure and

disappointment and disillusionment that in God's hands those things become polishing cloths for our grimy hearts?

I told a friend recently that I was writing about Peter and how, through his failure, he discovered the beauty of grace. She wrote right back: "Well, I just hate that! Why does it always have to be so hard?"

I smiled. I understand her reaction, don't you? In the end, Peter surely did, and the words of Christ from the Last Supper probably came back to haunt him. Peter may have remembered with regret at first, but then he heard Jesus' piercing love. What a gift to Peter that Jesus had prayed for him! Jesus knew that Peter would fail and prayed that, when Peter turned back, he would be able to strengthen the others. Peter would not understand grace until he tasted the bitterness of failure. In fact, his colossal failure to stand by Jesus taught Peter to find his strength and shelter in Christ.

Do you see the wonder in that? The Lord made it clear to Peter, first, that his failure would not disqualify him from being the leader Christ knew him to be and, second, that He, the Lord Himself, was praying for Peter.

It is easy in hindsight to see this opportunity for failure as a gift, but Peter didn't accept it as such. When Jesus told Peter that he would deny Him three times before the cock crowed, Peter was adamant that he would go to prison or even die before ever abandoning Christ.

I believe that Peter meant that with all his heart, but he was going to discover that, though his spirit was willing, his flesh was weak. God's ways are not our ways.

DON'T LIE DOWN LIKE A LAMB

When Jesus and the disciples left the room after their meal, they walked down to the Mount of Olives. When they arrived at the Garden, Jesus took Peter, James, and John aside with Him to pray. The three disciples tried to stay awake with Jesus, but sleep overcame them. Perhaps the meal and the wine or just the exhaustion of the previous few days overtook them. Though these disciples wanted to be there for Jesus, they could not help themselves.

Soon, a crowd of men rushed into the garden and chaos broke loose. Soldiers, officers from the chief priests, and

Pharisees had arrived brandishing torches, lanterns, and weapons that lighted up the night. Peter rose to his feet, pulled his sword from its sheath, and started swinging. He was doing all that he knew to stand with Christ, no matter what it cost him—even if it meant his life.

So when Jesus told him to put away his sword, Peter was shocked. Jesus had predicted just hours earlier that Peter would deny Him, and yet here Peter was ready to fight to the death for his Master. Peter must have been so confused: *Lord, I will fight for You! Don't expect me to just lie down like a lamb and take it!*

So when the Romans arrested Jesus and led Him away, Peter followed at a distance. Evil and hatred, fueled by all the powers of darkness, were in the air. As Peter stood in the courtyard of the high priests, he was recognized—not once, not twice, but three times. And each time, he denied knowing the Prisoner.

As dawn began to break, a cock crowed, and everything that was important to Peter, all he thought he brought to the table for Jesus, was shattered in the morning light.

THE PROMISE AMID THE MESS

We don't know what happened to Peter in the hours between his denials and the moment when he heard, after the Crucifixion, that Jesus' tomb was empty. He and the other disciples must have felt wretched and lonely. Where do you go when you have built your whole life on being strong, a man of your word, a leader, and then, when it counted most, you failed?

If you have taken your father's inheritance, broken his heart, spent all you had, and ended up feeding pigs, where do you go?

Peter would tell you and the prodigal would say, "Turn your heart toward home, toward God. Cling to His promise that He's got you covered with His lavish, unmerited grace. His power is made perfect in your weakness. Just recognize your need for the Shelter when you stand exposed and vulnerable."

Let's see what happened next.

It was very early on the morning after the Sabbath, after Jesus' murder, and Mary Magdalene, Mary the mother of James, and Salome went to the tomb to anoint Christ's body.

But the tomb was empty. Jesus' body was gone. An angel was present and he was terrifying, but he had a message. First, he calmed the women. "Don't be alarmed," he said (Mark 16:6)—but they were alarmed. Their shock increased when the angel told them that Christ had risen and said, "Go, tell his disciples and Peter, 'He is going ahead of you into Galilee. There you will see him, just as he told you'" (v. 7).

And Peter.

Do you hear the abundant grace in those two little words, two words that will mean everything to the impetuous disciple who feels he's messed up one time too many? God's messenger is clear: *make sure the one who thinks that he has failed knows that Jesus is waiting for him.*

The promise that was Peter's and the prodigal's is yours as well: "My grace is sufficient for you, for my power is made perfect in weakness" (2 Corinthians 12:9).

When Paul wrote, "My grace is sufficient," he wrote it in the present tense. He was saying, *Right now, at this very moment, whatever you are facing, God's grace is enough.* Paul's opponents wanted to see miracles as a sign that God was with him, but Paul turned that upside down and said, "No, it's in my very weakness that God shines and His strength holds me."

It's tempting to long for miracles and great power in our Christian walk that would show that God is with us and loves us, but the kingdom of God is no sideshow or three-ring circus. Rather, God is glorified when, in our weakness, we lean on His strength.

Do you feel that you have failed? That you are unloved? Without hope and beyond the point of salvation? Then join all of us who, when we expected to be put in our place, instead found a robe around our shoulders, a ring on our finger, and a party thrown to celebrate that we who once felt lost have been found. This is the glorious, outrageous way of the kingdom of God. He calls us to take another look in the mirror of His Word after we have fallen and failed. We brought before Him all we had, and not only was it not enough, but it tripped us up and sent us running into the night, feeling abandoned and alone.

But if you will listen for a moment, you will hear the party music that pierces your shame and calls all who are weak to find their strength in God alone. Grace doesn't tell us that our bad choices or failures don't matter; quite the reverse. Grace teaches us that our failures expose us for who we really are, and even as we are ready to count ourselves out, the cross casts its sheltering shadow over our broken hearts and welcomes us home.

Hope

God Said It;
I Believe It

GOD HAS SAID, "NEVER WILL
I LEAVE YOU; NEVER WILL
I FORSAKE YOU." SO WE SAY
WITH CONFIDENCE,
"THE LORD IS MY HELPER;
I WILL NOT BE AFRAID."

—HEBREWS 13:5–6

WHAT DO YOU WANT to be when you grow up? That frequently asked question gets us dreaming early on about what the future will be like. Maybe we imagine finding a cure for cancer or for the common cold. We fantasize about being the next Billy Graham or Mother Teresa. We consider the quiet joys of being a wife and a mom. We have beautiful visions of what can be and hope-filled expectations of how things should go. Then life gets hard. Losses threaten to strip us of hope rather than grow our faith. People leave us rather than arrive bearing gifts and good news. Suffering sits down, takes us firmly by the hand, and gives us a revised slide show of our life, and we're left feeling more alone in darkness than ever.

THE PROMISE OF HIS PRESENCE

How does God's promise never to leave us or forsake us—to be our Helper—fit into this real-life experience? Sometimes it's hard to understand. Even now, one of my greatest challenges when it comes to sharing my faith is a passionate commitment to tell the truth both about God's promises and about how hard life can be. Every day, so many of us wrestle with these contrary feelings:

- *I know that Jesus is the Way, but I feel lost.*
- *I know that He is my Healer, but I'm struggling with sickness.*
- *I know that all things work together for good to those who love God and are called according to His purpose, but I'm just not seeing how anything good will come out of this situation.*
- *I know that Christ promises peace, but I'm always anxious and frenzied.*

Our experiences with pain and struggle, trouble and hardship, do not diminish the promises of God at all. And we don't need to embellish those promises when we are sharing our faith as if we're God's PR agents. Sometimes we're confronted with a hard reality, and then God's promise to help us, to never leave us, suddenly feels false. Yet we pretend otherwise. We smile and say things are okay. We profess that God's promises must be true when in our hearts we're angry, confused, hurt, and feeling more alone than ever, because how could we doubt God's goodness and faithfulness?

The truth is, God doesn't want us to fake our faith or give lip service to His promises. No, He calls us to live with questions but drape them in assurance. Or, as my friend Randy Elrod says, God wants us to "be restless on the journey and confident in the destination."[1]

Dr. Helen Roseveare lived out this truth. In the hardest of circumstances, the most wrenching of events, Helen's life shows that God's promise of hope and comfort is real and true. Born in England in 1925, Helen started attending a prestigious all-girls school when she was just twelve years old and then

Cambridge, where she became a Christian. Her family went to church when she was a child, but she credits those she met through Christian Union at college with helping her understand the gospel for the first time. Impassioned to become a missionary, she focused on finishing her medical degree in order to use her skills and knowledge to help those most in need. At age twenty-eight, she set sail for the Belgian Congo (now known as the Democratic Republic of the Congo) with Worldwide Evangelical Crusade (WEC).

However, the rose-tinted horizon Helen saw quickly darkened. In her book *Give Me This Mountain*, she tells of immediate resistance to her efforts to train the locals in health care and how men at the mission post failed to give her, a young single woman, respect. She found herself feeling frustrated and at times angry.[2] These things, however, would be the least of her worries, for no missionary training program could have prepared her for what she would face one day in 1964.

She remembered hearing a truck come into the village and rough shouts in the streets. The war in the Congo had begun. Two men burst into Helen's home, destroyed many of her possessions, beat her, broke her glasses—leaving her unable to see and feeling even more helpless—and violated her throughout the night. Helen wrote, "I don't think I was praying; I was numb with horror, dread, fear. If I had prayed, I think I would have prayed, 'My God, my God, why hast thou forsaken me?' I felt He's left me. I didn't doubt God. I never doubted God. But I felt, for that moment, that He'd left me to handle the situation by myself."[3]

Have you ever been there? Have you walked through a situation so painful and lonely that it seems as if you are completely on your own? Perhaps you have a chronically sick child, and with each rushed trip to the emergency room, you wonder if God is there or if you have to get through this one by yourself. Or maybe you are fighting to hold together your marriage, doing all you can, but it doesn't seem as if God is doing much to support you.

Many men and women in Scripture felt that way:

- Gideon wondered, "If the LORD is with us, why has all this happened to us? Where are all his wonders that our fathers told us about when they said, 'Did not the LORD bring us out of Egypt?' But now the LORD has abandoned us and put us into the hand of Midian" (Judges 6:13).

- Job cried out, "Why did I not perish at birth, and die as I came from the womb?" (Job 3:11).

- David pleaded, "Why, O LORD, do you stand far off? Why do you hide yourself in times of trouble?" (Psalm 10:1). And, "My God, my God, why have you forsaken me? Why are you so far from saving me, so far from the words of my groaning? O my God, I cry out by day, but you do not answer, by night, and am not silent" (22:1–2).

- And echoing verses from Psalm 22, even Christ on the cross cried out loudly in pain, 'Eloi, Eloi, lama sabachthani?'—which means, "My God, my God, why have you forsaken me?" (Mark 15:34).

The experience of walking through a dark night is a common bond for those who love God. But the redemption of this struggle is the ability to turn to those who will follow in your path and let them know they are not alone. There is a comfort

Suffering and comfort walk hand in hand, in that we belong to the God who both suffers with us and brings comfort...

that only the One who has walked through the night into the morning can bring to another person who is still in the darkness.

So it was for Dr. Helen Roseveare, who—along with other missionaries—was held captive by rebel forces for five months. She wrote about how God used her own brutal rapes to enable her to offer comfort to other missionaries. Some of these women feared that, since they had lost their virginity due to a rape, they might have lost their salvation too. Helen knew otherwise. She knew that her relationship with God had not been damaged. She had not failed God in any way. For these women who suffered, Helen's words were credible only because of what she herself had been through.

The comfort Helen gave others grew

out of her own pain and trauma. One of my favorite passages of Scripture found in 2 Corinthians says it best: "Praise be to the God and Father of our Lord Jesus Christ, the Father of compassion and the God of all comfort, who comforts us in all our troubles, so that we can comfort those in any trouble with the comfort we ourselves have received from God. For just as the sufferings of Christ flow over into our lives, so also through Christ our comfort overflows" (1:3–5).

Suffering and comfort walk hand in hand, in that we belong to the God who both suffers with us *and* brings comfort, care, and understanding to us. In fact, He brings His very self.

That idea has changed my understanding of the promises of Christ. God makes us this promise: "Never will I leave you; never will I forsake you" (Hebrews 13:5). The Scripture doesn't say we will never hurt, but rather that we will never be alone in that hurt. We can be sure to say, then, "The Lord is my helper; I will not be afraid" (v. 6).

God's promises are a stronger foundation for life than our feelings are. His promises are sound and sure, the stuff to nail your heart to in the worst travails of life. Dr. Helen Roseveare's life illustrates that even when you don't feel God's presence, you can be assured He is there and you can know His comfort and hope.

ℒOOKING FOR HOPE

If ever a woman needed God's presence and Christ's comfort, it was Mary Magdalene. She was the tormented soul possessed by not just one but seven demons when she met Jesus, her Deliverer, somewhere along the shores of the Sea of Galilee (Luke 8:1–3). We know that Mary came from a noble family and that her hometown was Magdala, on the northwest shore of the Sea of Galilee. Although we don't know details of her healing or her face-to-face encounter with Jesus, we do know that He banished the powers of darkness from her life. Being brought from such a dark life into one of light and peace— would that not change everything, would that not make you want to linger with the source of that light and dwell in it the rest of your days?

After all, when heaven invades your hell, it wins your heart's allegiance. That was true for Mary Magdalene, and that truth must be what drew her to the cross. We do not see her again in the Gospels until the crucifixion, burial, and resurrection of Christ—and she is not only there, but she figures prominently in the account. Near the cross of Jesus, Mary stood with His mother, His mother's sister, and Mary the wife of Clopas (John 19:25). These women heard Jesus cry, "My God, my God, why have you forsaken me?" These women were there when a strange darkness covered the earth at noon. And when the darkness fell, there was silence. Christ became sin, and His Father turned away from Him as He bore the sin of the world. Even in our darkest moments, we will never know the agony of all Christ endured so that we will never have to be alone.

And Mary Magdalene heard it all. She stayed by Jesus through the persecution and at the cross. She was there when He cried out, "It is finished." Then she followed His body to the grave and lingered there.

$\mathcal{I}$T'S OVER WHEN GOD SAYS IT'S OVER

The Jewish authorities who had plotted to have Christ crucified intended to make sure that all rumors of a resurrection died with Jesus. By getting Rome to assign an official military guard to the site where the slain Jesus was entombed, the powerful Jewish Sanhedrin had a round-the-clock watch at the burial place.

But an earthquake threw open the tomb, and the sleeping soldiers faced the unthinkable reality that Jesus' body was missing. The guards passed out from sheer terror, which was just as well, as this moment did not belong to them (Matthew 28:2–4). This moment had been planned for Mary before she was even born.

Night turned to morning, but before morning broke on that third day, Mary hurried to the tomb to anoint Christ's body. It had been buried quickly to get it to a place of rest before sundown on Friday, the beginning of the Sabbath, and now Mary wanted to take care of it properly. When she arrived, she was surprised to see that the stone had been moved and then horrified to learn that someone had taken Christ's body.

When Peter and John looked inside the tomb, they saw that it was empty and that the grave clothes were wrapped and lying there. They believed and went home (John 20:8–10), but Mary stayed and wept.

Then, bending over to look into the tomb once again, she saw two angels seated where Jesus' body had been. They asked her,

"Woman, why are you crying?"

"They have taken my Lord away," she said, "and I don't know where they have put him." At this, she turned around and saw Jesus standing there, but she did not realize that it was Jesus.

He asked her, "Woman, why are you crying? Who is it you are looking for?"

Thinking he was the gardener, she said, "Sir, if you have carried him away, tell me where you have put him, and I will get him."

Jesus said to her, "Mary."

She turned toward him and cried out in Aramaic, "Rabboni!" (which means Teacher). (John 20:13–16)

There is nothing more beautiful than your name on the lips of the one you love. How much more so to hear Christ utter your name when you thought you had lost Him forever. How gracious of Jesus to save this moment—this first sighting of His resurrected body by any man, woman, or child—for Mary. This woman who had been tormented by the demons of hell was blessed to see the victorious Christ. He had defeated darkness once and for all, and He allowed one who had been there too to be the first to celebrate the victory with Him.

So, we hold on to God's promise that He will never leave us, never forsake us. Even in our darkest night, He is there. Christ brings life from death. And your Father takes nothing that you are walking through lightly. He will use your hard times and struggles, and He will use you to bring comfort and healing to another broken heart. You can be sure when you say, "I will not be afraid because the Lord is my Helper." Time after time, I have heard these same words from women who have walked through devastating times: "I never would have signed up for this, but I know Christ now at a depth and with an intimacy that I never knew was possible." The hope Christ promises becomes more real because of the trials He brings us through.

Ask Dr. Helen Roseveare. Ask Mary Magdalene. You could certainly ask me, and I would tell you: Jesus is light, the glory of God. He is grace, an amazing gift. He is the cleft in the rock into which you can retreat when you're broken and weary. You will find understanding in His shelter and hope in His presence. He will wrap His arms around you and hold your faint heart with His nail-scarred hands. He will be there. Always.

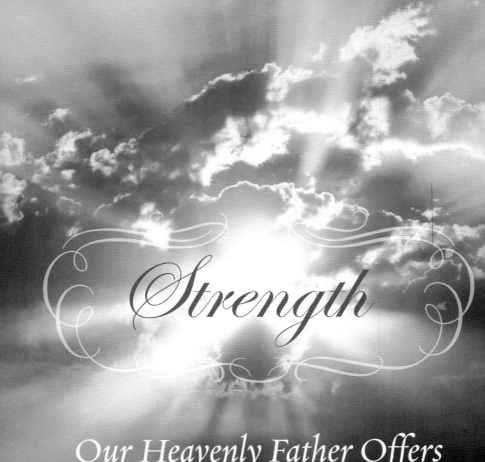

Strength

Our Heavenly Father Offers
the Sacrament of Suffering

"In this world you will have trouble. But take heart! I have overcome the world."

—John 16:33

I FIRST MET JONI EARECKSON TADA (she was just Joni Eareckson then) in 1983 at a Christian festival in Holland. We looked into each other's eyes and talked for a while. We knew we would be friends.

Maybe you know Joni's story. She was a young woman when she broke her neck in a diving accident. And one of the great sadnesses and ironies of Joni's life is that even though she is paralyzed from the neck down, she still suffers considerable pain. You would think that paralysis means an absence of pain, that you feel nothing, but Joni has not been given that relief. The strength that I always see in her is not a timid thing. Celebrating Christ in the midst of her reality has been and continues to be a brutal battle each day. Yet each day she relentlessly puts on her internal boxing gloves and fights.

When I interviewed Joni on *The 700 Club* television show in 1991, I became even more aware of a dimension in her relationship with Jesus—an iron core of strength that was both intangible and yet undeniably real. At the time, I couldn't have told you what this dimension was. I just knew I wanted it. I wanted to know what she knew. I wanted the relationship she had with Christ. Clearly, Joni had lived a life of suffering. Was suffering the key, the thing that birthed this quality that I couldn't quite define? I didn't want the suffering—who does?— but I did want the knowing she possessed. And the strength.

So when I said good-bye to Joni that first day we met, I determined to stay in touch and to grow our friendship. Then in 1992, my life fell apart, and I lost touch with everyone.

THE PROMISE OF STRENGTH

As I sat in the psychiatrist's office in the hospital, I could hear him talking to me, but it was as if I were listening through glass or trapped inside a goldfish bowl. His eyes were kind, and his posture as he leaned forward seemed to invite trust, but I was done with that. He talked to me about recent gains in understanding clinical depression and new medications that were more efficient at arresting that crushing feeling of disappearing a little bit more each day. I could tell that he was offering me hope, but I wasn't taking it.

It's not that I saw him as anything other than the fine doctor he proved to be. I just wasn't interested. He offered the first few steps on a path to recovery and wellness, and I didn't want it. The *drip, drip, drip* of depression had taken its toll until I finally felt as if I were drowning, and I had no strength or desire left to fight. I felt as if I were going under. Even though this doctor was throwing me a life preserver, I didn't have the energy or desire to grab hold of it.

I find it strange now as I sit at my kitchen table, typing

these words, to step back into that place of utter darkness and despair. It seems like another life. I look out the window and watch my fourteen-year-old son throwing a football with his dad and marvel that at one point I wanted to die.

A friend recently suggested that I should see my depression as part of my past and not talk about it anymore: "After all, you don't want to be the poster child for depression, do you?"

I'm not sure. Perhaps I do. Not in terms of being stuck in the past and unable to get on with my life, but certainly in being present and available for those just beginning their dark descent. Depression is a very isolating disease, which only adds to the despair. I want others to know what I discovered—that help and healing are available and that one day you will actually want community and crave not just the company of others but closeness, too. It doesn't happen overnight, but every step in the right direction lifts the darkness just a little.

I also discovered that God has tucked something holy into suffering. I wouldn't even attempt to say what suffering might look like or feel like for you at this moment, but let me say that as I fell off the edge of my life, I discovered that I had always been held. In some mysterious way it was as if God reached out, grabbed hold of me, and lifted me. I was physically weak and emotionally worn out, but aware of the seeds of that something that I had seen deep in Joni's eyes. Initially I wanted to run from the powerlessness of dangling and hanging on to God and His promises. I didn't want to be vulnerable or feel out of control. After all, I had taught myself well through the years to take care of myself so that no one would be able to hurt me too deeply. But I discovered that when I protect myself from people, I shield myself from God, too.

Key to tapping into the power of allowing Christ to help you through your troubles and sufferings is to finally come to the end of yourself and decide, no matter the cost, that you want to be free to love Christ and follow Him wherever He leads. Even if it means going to a place where the only thing that keeps you from falling into confusion or despair is grasping His promise to overcome *for you*. I had to decide in the psych ward that I no longer wanted to live a safe, comfortable, cold life. I wanted to live abandoned to God. I began to see that too often I was only willing to give God as much as I could afford to lose. But God does not intend for us to live careful lives, holding back who we really are, being quiet about our hopes and fears. True strength invites us to live with an open heart and soul, knowing that Christ has a good, strong hold on us.

For me, strength meant resigning from my self-imposed position as my own savior and embracing becoming a lamb following her Shepherd.

So now when I feel myself pulling away from my closest friends, I choose to reach out and ask them to pray for me rather than retreating into a dark place.

Or when I am aware of someone walking through the nightmare of, say, a child with cancer, I pull in close to her to reinforce that she is not alone because I know that even in her place Christ is present in the sacrament of suffering.

It is one thing to say, "The LORD is my shepherd, I shall not be in want." It is quite another when you find yourself in a dark place and discover that you *are* not alone—when you truly begin to rely on God's promise that is tucked into Psalm 23:4: "Even though I walk through the valley of the shadow of death, I will fear no evil, for you are with me; your rod and your staff, they comfort me."

My falling off the edge looked like this: one day I was the co-host of a nationally syndicated talk show, and that night I was a patient in a psychiatric ward. Quite a reversal of fortunes. And I thought about Joni. She didn't choose the life she now had. She dove off a platform and broke her neck. I am not for one moment beginning to compare the suffering that Joni continues to experience with anything I have known. But I knew enough of the struggles she faced to know how tempting it is to simply want to opt out of the days and weeks ahead.

Climbing back out of a deep hole is hard, and there are many painful truths to face as you make the climb. If you have never suffered from serious depression, I think it's hard to understand the physical and mental pain involved. Much of depression is silent and isolating and . . . within. A brain tumor shows up on a CT scan, but depleted brain chemicals do not. So the temptation for those who are looking on is to say, "Pull yourself together. You have so much to be thankful for!" To those who are in the eye of the storm, that is like saying to a child with a crushed leg, "Get up and walk."

The quiet strength I saw in Joni was borne out of the crucible of pain that runs so deep you cannot move, a crucible of grief so overwhelming it crushes you with the weight of an ocean. But what Joni found is that when you are pinned, you are held. And that reality has given her an intimacy with Christ that is simply beautiful.

I don't speak of these things lightly. As you read these words, you might be in the middle of unimaginable grief. I want you to remember—or know for the first time—that Christ has been to the bottom of the pit of grief. He tasted the worst dregs that hell can pour out, and He rose again to set us free and secure for us a destiny with Him forever—a destiny that Satan cannot touch. As each of us walks on our unique path that will take us to that eternal home, He promises to walk with us and to help us overcome.

By the time Joni and I met a second time, I was in a totally different place spiritually from when we first met. I was beginning to understand what Scripture calls "the treasures of darkness" (Isaiah 45:3). Joni saw that. She told me that when

TRUE STRENGTH

*invites us to live with
an open heart and soul,
knowing that*

Christ

HAS A GOOD

STRONG HOLD ON US.

she met me, the first word that came to her mind was *strong*. After my hospitalization, she said, "A different and even better word came to mind: *gentle*. More so, *broken and gentle*."

No matter what circumstances pull the carpet out from underneath us, I have found, like millions before me who have walked this path of faith, that God will use the darkest of nights to let us know that He is there and that He upholds us. Christ's words that we have known for years suddenly take on new life and breath. They take on genuine hope. Jesus told those closest to Him, *You are going to have trouble in this world. That is a given. Don't be surprised by it or look anymore for a trouble-free life. Take heart! Strengthen yourself with this absolute truth: I have overcome the world. We win; it's a sure thing. So when you can't hold on any longer, know this: I am holding you. When your strength runs out, I've still got you in My grip, and I'll give you My strength to hold on to.*

That is quite a promise. And Jesus' disciples were about to find out just what it meant.

A REVOLUTION FOR THE WEAK

When Jesus made His promise to overcome the world (John 16:33), His disciples were thinking that things just might be looking up for them and their people. They didn't see that Jesus' life as a man was just hours away from crashing down around Him or that He was about to spend His final night with His friends. They went to the Upper Room and prepared to have supper. But first Jesus needed to give them one final lesson. He grabbed a towel, then a water basin, and began to wash His disciples' feet.

The disciples were stunned. Their would-be king had just taken on the most demeaning, menial job, one reserved for non-Jewish slaves. The Most Powerful had chosen the place of the lowliest. Jesus chose to spend His final hours on earth in a role of weakness and humility, not overcoming. Had the disciples understood just how little sand was left to run through the hourglass, they might have asked, *This is overcoming the world?*

Maybe you are asking that even now.

It's a good question, and Jesus' answer was revolutionary:

[Jesus] grabbed a towel, then a water basin, and began to wash His disciples' feet.

In weakness there is strength. God's plan, from the very beginning, was to overcome the world not with force, but with love, a violent love stronger than death, a love that waters cannot quench or rivers overflow (Song of Solomon 8:6–7).

As he started his account of the footwashing scene, John wrote this: "Having loved his own who were in the world, he now showed them the full extent of his love" (John 13:1). In washing His dear friends' feet, Jesus gave them and us a taste of what He was about to do for all of us—to wash us clean, using His very blood. In fact, all the way from Genesis to Revelation, since we are unable to cover ourselves, Christ covers us by the washing of His blood.

The One who spoke everything into being chose to bend His knee and allow the sin of the world to crush Him so that we could be free and His Father would be glorified (Philippians 2:7–11). The disciples did not understand this in the Upper Room as Jesus was washing their feet. And that was when Jesus showed them—and us—one of the most remarkable things about His promise to help us overcome the world and exactly how He was going to keep that promise.

*H*IS PRAYERS KEEP THE PROMISE

First, Jesus told His disciples some disturbing things:

- *To Peter, "You will betray Me."*
- *To the whole table, "Just as the world hates Me, it will hate you too."*
- *"You all will be thrown out of the synagogue. In fact, a time is coming when those who put Christ's followers to death will believe that they are doing it for God" (John 16:1–2).*
- *And that on this very night, when Jesus needed His friends the most, "You will scatter to your homes and abandon Me."*

Do these words sound like the way to strengthen the faint of heart or empower the weak? *What is Jesus doing?*

I believe He was saying, *All of this will happen, but God is still in control.* He was telling Peter, *When you hear yourself doing the very thing you swore you would never do, I understand and I love you.* He was telling His disciples then and us now, *When your world falls apart and nothing makes sense anymore, you are still being held. Nothing that happens will be a surprise to God.*

Having spoken these words, Jesus led His closest disciples to the Mount of Olives. And while the disciples slept, exhausted and spent, Jesus prayed: "Father, if you are willing, take this cup from me; yet not my will, but yours be done" (Luke 22:42). Here Christ brought together our humanity and the call to servanthood. Knowing the trouble that lay ahead of Him that night, Christ asked if it was possible to have it removed, yet in the same breath He bowed His knee to God's will.

Before they had left the Upper Room that night, Jesus prayed for his friends: "My prayer is not that you take them out of the world but that you protect them from the evil one" (John 17:15). God will "protect" us, as the verse says. How remarkable—and how giving. In His own moment of uncertainty and grief, profound sadness and fatigue, Jesus asked His Father not to remove us from the world and its troubles, but to protect us, to give us strength and endurance and resilience.

Jesus knew what was coming for Him, yet He stopped to pray for His disciples, for you, and for me. What a powerful example. His very actions show us that we can face suffering best by not giving in to it or pulling in to ourselves, but by reaching out and looking up and holding on to this promise: trouble is knit into the very fabric of this life, but Christ has overcome. The one thing we all know for sure is that, to one degree or another, each of us will suffer in this world. Some people have to bear far more than others. Some may appear to glide through life pain-free, but no one escapes unscathed. No matter how hard the circumstances, Jesus assures the faint of heart that He has overcome the world and He will help us do the same—and the timing of that promise is important. Just hours before Jesus was to be betrayed by His friends, mocked and beaten, flogged and tortured, nailed to a cross and spit upon—murdered—His heart-to-heart message to His closest friends is this: *take heart, I have overcome the world.*

In the moments of our deepest grief. His arms are wide open to us, strong enough to keep us and strong enough to lift us from this world.

All of Christ's promises are deeply comforting, but in this one promise I hear a battle cry. As I look at the trail that Christ blazed for you and me so that we could be free to love Him and live with Him forever, I want, even in the midst of trouble, to stand. No matter how alone we may feel at times, because of what Jesus has done on the cross for us, we are never alone. Even in the eye of a storm, we call our hearts to remember that, no matter how hard life gets, we win!

HIS ARMS ARE

wide open to us,

STRONG ENOUGH TO KEEP US

*and strong enough to
lift us from this world.*

Why Am I
Settling for Less?

More

....

"ASK AND IT WILL BE GIVEN TO YOU;

SEEK AND YOU WILL FIND; KNOCK

AND THE DOOR WILL BE OPENED TO

YOU. FOR EVERYONE WHO ASKS

RECEIVES; HE WHO SEEKS FINDS;

AND TO HIM WHO KNOCKS, THE

DOOR WILL BE OPENED."

—MATTHEW 7:7–8

....

I CAN STILL SEE their faces and the big cheesy grins that swept from ear to ear. Christian and his friend Chase sat up in their twin beds like little princes with the room service menus in hand.

After a few moments of reviewing the menu, Christian popped his head around the door. "Can I order for Chase and me?" he asked. "I know what to do! Please?"

"Okay," I said, and he dashed back to his buddy.

"So you've done this before?" Chase asked.

"Hundreds of times," Christian replied.

"And we don't need money?" Chase prodded.

"No, dude, it's like a miracle," Christian answered. "You just call up and order whatever you want, and they bring it up on a tray and you just sign a piece of paper and that's it."

I waited until I heard the knock on their door and then watched what happened. Christian dutifully signed the check, and I showed the server out. When I turned around, I saw for the first time what they had actually ordered: two large pepperoni pizzas—one for each of them, a pint of ice cream, and a pot of hot chocolate.

"Look at all this, Mom," Christian announced triumphantly. "And it didn't cost us a thing!"

That night I explained the inner workings of room service to my son and his mesmerized friend. I told them that, yes, there are wonderful things for the asking—and, no, you do not receive if you do not ask—but there really is no such thing as a free lunch! Later, as I reflected back on that evening, it both horrified and amused me to think that they could have just gone down the whole menu and ordered everything on there! Instead, they went for good ol' boy food. Then I wondered if, in many ways, we do something similar in our relationship with

God. Our heavenly Father offers us so much more than a room service menu, and His resources are unlimited! But like Christian and his friend, we sometimes settle for ordering junk food instead of the bountiful gourmet meal God offers of His presence in every moment of our lives.

A PROMISE OF MORE

Too often we settle for small, temporal things in place of the great spiritual wealth God waits to give us. No wonder that at the end of the Sermon on the Mount, Jesus gives this promise, "Ask and it will be given to you; seek and you will find; knock and the door will be opened to you. For everyone who asks receives; he who seeks finds; and to him who knocks, the door will be opened" (Matthew 7:7–8).

On first read you might be tempted to think this promise plays into our more self-indulgent side, but let's dig deep and find the treasure awaiting us. What Jesus is promising is a radical transformation in how we think and how we live. His promise to us, like that sermon, is about more: whatever we ask, He has more in store. What He is about to say will change everything if we understand the promise.

Certainly the people on that hillside didn't expect what Jesus was going to say that day. He would tell them it was the heart that mattered and then say that, because of the heart, we should live with more abandon and passion. He would tell the people that God is not distant or disapproving or disconnected, but a Father who loves to give good gifts to His children. So they should ask and ask and keep on asking.

LEAN IN AND LISTEN

To understand how striking Jesus' promise is, put yourself in the place of the people who first heard it. The Sermon on the Mount was no simple sermon of niceties. There was shock and awe. Jesus didn't ease into the teaching or begin with a lovely greeting. He blew them away.

In fact, the first word out of Christ's mouth riveted the crowd because it was a word never associated with them: *blessed*. This powerful word, meaning "divine joy, perfect happiness," described the kind of joy believed only to be experienced by the gods or the dead.[1] *Blessed* also implied an inner security and rest that didn't depend on outward circumstances or an ability to keep rules. This was so much more than the Jews could have hoped for. They strived to be acceptable, to escape judgment—but to be blessed? What a gift!

And what a revolutionary concept to Jesus' audience! The Pharisees, their intellectual and zealous gatekeepers, had taught them that righteousness is tied to external behavior, that it is a matter of obeying rules and regulations, of which there were many. The Pharisees had taught that praying, giving, fasting, and keeping all the other dietary and Sabbath rules indicated one's righteousness.

But in the Beatitudes, Jesus described how character flows from within the human heart. He did not provide a list of tasks to tick off by the end of the day but rather a radical new way to live: sold out to God. Jesus called people to join a new kingdom that would cost them everything they had—and would give them everything they needed. Imagine spending your whole life trying to keep every little nitpicky rule in an attempt to find favor with God—and suddenly hearing that what really matters is your heart!

JESUS RAISES THE BAR

Do you see how complicated and stressful life was for the Jewish people? What a relief then when Jesus spoke, and the first word out of His mouth was *blessed*. Even more astonishing was His list of specific people who are blessed: the poor in spirit, those who mourn, the meek, those who hunger and thirst for righteousness, the merciful, the pure in heart, the peacemakers, those who are persecuted for righteousness' sake, and those who are reviled or persecuted on account of Christ (Matthew 5:1–12).

I can imagine the crowd being initially stunned but then heartened by Jesus' promise of a blessed life. These listeners were a persecuted people, after all. The Romans ruled over their lives and taxed them into poverty. They even used some of their own Jewish people to extract ridiculous taxes and turned a blind eye to those who took more than was required and pocketed the rest. I'm sure there was no more despised group of people than the Jews who worked for the Romans and used the power of the Roman boot to line their own pockets.

One of these men was Zacchaeus. His name means "pure," but his life belied his name: he'd become rich at the expense of those around him. But Zacchaeus discovered that there is something intrinsically disappointing built into everything this world offers and what he really needed only Jesus could give him. Zacchaeus had connived his way into great wealth, but he knew utter spiritual poverty. He was starving to death for what mattered, for what would last. In a dramatic encounter with Christ, Zacchaeus received more than he had ever dared to ask or dream. We'll look at his story in a moment.

Not only had the Romans oppressed the Jewish people, but the leaders sent by God to guide and love His people had worn them into the ground with their petty rules and regulations. They offered no joy or grace or freedom, just a merciless yardstick that told the story of how far short each Jew fell every single day. And then came a Man who spoke out against this oppression.

But Jesus' message got more complicated when He dropped this bombshell: "Unless your righteousness surpasses that of the Pharisees and the teachers of the law, you will certainly not enter the kingdom of heaven" (Matthew 5:20).

Can you imagine the people thinking, *Okay, Lord, You had me for a bit there, but now You've lost me completely! First of all, You tell me that what matters is my heart, but then You tell me that unless my righteousness exceeds those who have been holding these laws over our lives, I'm not getting into heaven? That gives me no hope at all.*

$\mathcal{L}$IVE HIGHER, LEAN HARDER

Having initially brought much-needed comfort and hope to the crowd on the hill that day, Jesus then presented the people with an impossible task: to keep the letter of the law even more completely than the most devout Jewish leader did. It was as if He delivered directly to the people the most wonderful room service, bringing just what they needed, with greater richness than they even imagined, and then reminded them there is a high price to pay.

How can we do that? the people must have thought, when Jesus said to keep the law even beyond the letter, to the heart. *How can we live this impossible demand?*

Their religious leaders were supposed to bring them comfort

and hope. Instead, the Pharisees had done nothing but add to the harshness of life for the people. And now this Jesus, who had spoken so comfortingly to them, was talking about not only living out the letter of the law, but way beyond it.

The people must have been spent.

And that's when Jesus did the most remarkable thing yet. Looking at the crowd—I can only imagine the love contained in His eyes—He said, "Do not worry about your life." He promised that the Father cares for us and waits for us to come to Him when we are lost, when we need direction, or when we are longing for answers.

So at the end of this long and, at times, confusing sermon comes this outrageous promise that invites us not to expect less but rather to ask for much more from a Father who loves us and knows our real needs: "Ask and it will be given to you; seek and you will find; knock and the door will be opened to you. For everyone who asks receives; he who seeks finds; and to him who knocks, the door will be opened" (Matthew 7:7–8).

The original Greek indicates that Jesus was saying, *Shout to God. Run to Him. Bang on His door anytime, day or night, and you will find*

God there, always ready, ever waiting to give you even beyond what you need.

ARE OUR DESIRES TOO WEAK?

This is an incredible message! Jesus not only reminds us that God waits to give to us what we seek and has an ever-open door for the asking, but that He will deliver beyond what we even know we want or need. I love the way C. S. Lewis put it in *The Weight of Glory*: "We are half-hearted creatures, fooling about with drink and sex and ambition when infinite joy is offered us, like an ignorant child who wants to go on making mud pies in a slum because he cannot imagine what is meant by the offer of a holiday at the sea. We are far too easily pleased."[2]

ASK, SEEK, KNOCK FOR WHAT?

At the end of the Sermon on the Mount comes an invitation that Christ tied directly to what every father in the crowd would understand—that most primal desire to provide for one's children:

"Which of you, if his son asks for bread, will give him a stone? Or if he asks for a fish, will give him a snake? If you, then, though you are evil, know how to give good gifts to your children, how much more will your Father in heaven give good gifts to those who ask him!" (Matthew 7:9–11).

It might be reasonable for someone in the listening crowd to ask, "How do we know that's true?" The powerful analogy of our heavenly Father's relationship with us and the relationship between an earthly father and son helps answer that question. In Matthew we read, "Which of you, if his son asks for bread, will give him a stone? Or if he asks for a fish, will give him a snake?" Luke adds, "Or if he asks for an egg, will he give him a scorpion?" (11:12). These are unlikely pairings to us, but Jesus' audience would have a clear picture of what that would look like. The small, round limestone rocks on the sea-

God waits to give to us what we seek and has an ever-open door for the asking...

shore would look exactly like the small loaves of bread a mother would put in her son's lunch box. So Jesus asks, "What father would trick his son and, instead of giving him the bread he needs, swap it out for a stone?"

The next question is, "What father would give his boy a serpent if he asked for a fish?" The serpent alluded to would almost certainly be an eel, which according to Jewish dietary laws was unclean (Leviticus 11:12).

Next up, the scorpion and the egg. When a scorpion is folded up and at rest, the pale ones look exactly like an egg but in reality would be terrifying to a child. The scorpion's sting is very painful and can even be deadly.

Jesus was saying that if those of us who are part of this fallen, broken world wouldn't give a child something he couldn't eat or something that would scare and harm him, how much more will God, who knows us and loves us, run to meet our needs? God's love for us is so far above what we think we need, and His answers spring out of the depth of His love, mercy, and wisdom.

NOT ONCE, NOT TWICE, BUT OVER AND OVER

When we read *ask*, *seek*, *knock* in Matthew 7:7–8, it is good to know that those commands mean never stop asking, never stop seeking, and never stop knocking. God fully knows us and loves us, so we go to our Father as children who are dearly loved and we ask, ask, and keep on asking! God, out of the depth of His grace and love, gives us so much more than we would even know to ask for.

Just ask Zacchaeus.

FROM AN OUTCAST TO A PLACE OF HONOR

Zacchaeus the tax collector had become a very wealthy man in Jericho, a significant center of commerce stationed along a major trade route. We are not told anything about Zacchaeus's personal life, whether he was married or had children, but one thing is clear: he was not a happy man. He had everything we are often told will make us happy, but it was not enough.

So what happens if you have all the things that you are told will make you happy . . . and they don't? I think that was the life Zacchaeus led until one day he heard that this man Jesus was coming through Jericho.

Zacchaeus was determined to find out what all the fuss was about this man. He took off and, interestingly, became one who was asking and seeking and knocking. He ran ahead of the crowd and climbed up into a tree, knowing that his slight stature would make it hard for him to see over the crowd. He could never have known that God was looking for him, too.

When Jesus looked up into the tree and addressed Zacchaeus by name, I bet he almost fell out of the tree! Then Jesus did something that no other Jew would have done: He went to Zacchaeus's home, and that changed the tax collector's life for eternity.

So MUCH MORE

Zacchaeus gave half of what he had to the poor, and to those he had cheated, he gave the amount back to them fourfold. Church history tells us that Zacchaeus went on to become the bishop of Caesarea. He who wanted a glimpse of God became His honored servant. Zacchaeus experienced more than he ever thought possible.

As I think back to those two little boys marveling over the magic of a room service menu and how radical it was to order a whole pizza each, I think God looks down at us and says, *My child, don't settle for what will feed you for a moment. Ask for more! There is so much more I want to give you. You long to know My presence, and I long to reveal Myself to you . . . if you would just ask. You seek happiness in places that bring only disappointment and pain, but if you seek Me, I will be found, and you will be filled. You knock timidly at My door, and I say knock with everything that is in you, and I will throw the doors of heaven open. I call you to My side. I AM your shelter.*

Hear Him answer your call:

- ❧ *If you ask, I will answer.*
- ❧ *If you seek, you will find.*
- ❧ *If you knock, I will open the door.*
- ❧ *There is more. There is so much more!*

Now to him who is able to

do immeasurably more

than all we ask or imagine,

according to his power that

is at work within us...

EPHESIANS 3:20

Home

The Shelter Is Complete

"In my Father's house are many rooms; if it were not so, I would have told you. I am going there to prepare a place for you."

—John 14:2

I WAS NOT ONE OF THOSE GIRLS who had always longed for motherhood. The thought of taking care of such a fragile human being was daunting to me. I thought of myself as more of a cat-and-dog mother.

And, at thirty-nine, I had made peace with the reality that, most likely, I would never be the mother of a child. Barry and I had married later in life. We tried for a few months, and I gave it my full attention—but the plus sign never appeared. I decided that I didn't want to get entrenched in that monthly ritual of hope and disappointment, so I set the issue on the back shelf of my mind.

Well, you know the saying: when you stop pursuing something, that's often the time it arrives. A few weeks later I was aware of being a little more tired than normal. I felt a little queasy when I woke up. Yet

I didn't put two and two together. Not until one day, when I was cleaning out my bathroom cabinet and saw that I still had one pregnancy testing kit left over from the jumbo box I had purchased at Costco. I almost threw it in the trash, but on a whim I thought I'd take it. I took the test and put it on the window ledge and forgot all about it. Later that afternoon, I saw it and, a little horrified that I'd just left it sitting there, picked it up and threw it in the trash. I remember that moment as if it happened in slow motion. As the test stick fell into the trash, it spun a couple of times, and something caught my eye. It landed result-side down in the bottom of the freshly cleaned-out trash can.

Did I just see a plus sign?

I realize that most of you would have immediately grabbed the thing and turned it over, but I didn't. I sat on the floor beside the can and peered in. Being pregnant, having a baby of my own, would change everything in my world. I picked the stick out of the trash and sat it on the floor, still result-side down.

"Well, Lord, if this is negative, You just don't have it in Your plan for me to be a mother, and that's probably a good thing, as I did drop the watermelon and the cat. If, on the other hand, it is positive, You will help me, right? You can help me to hold on to a baby, right?"

With that, I turned over the test stick and there it was: positive!

I cried for a long time.

Then I danced my way into the spare room that would be my little one's new home.

THE PROMISE OF A TRUE HOME

It was one thing for me, at age thirty-nine with a penchant for dropping things, to discover that I was going to have a baby. But can you even begin to imagine what it must have been like for Mary, the mother of Jesus? Her life and world open up to us one of the most beautiful promises of God, the Ultimate Promise, the promise of eternity with Him, because He is our home.

Jesus' promise to us before His execution—"I am going . . . to prepare a place for you" (John 14:2)—would have unique significance and power for Mary. The mother of Jesus had not been able to prepare much of a place for this little one the night He was born. Perhaps she wondered if anything she had been able to give Him was enough. . . .

Girls in Mary's time were betrothed or engaged when they were twelve or thirteen. It was not an engagement as we know it—one that could be broken off at any point up until the wedding with no legal ramifications. No, this was a formal bond that could be broken only by a decree of divorce and that usually lasted for a year, during which time no sexual activity was to take place. The penalty for any immorality occurring during the engagement was death by stoning for the man and the virgin (Deuteronomy 22:23–24).

Do you see the enormity of what was happening in Mary's life? That God chose her for this assignment shows us a lot about the kind of girl she was and the kind of man Joseph was. They went through a lot as they waited for the Messiah to come to their home in order to make a way for all of us to find the way back to our one true home, to heaven for an eternity with Christ.

HOW COULD IT END LIKE THIS?

Since we all know how the story ends, let's start there. Everything within Mary wanted to fall to the dry ground that was absorbing His blood like a ravenous animal. Rather, she stood and never took her eyes off His face, watching as He struggled to breathe. How she longed to hold Him one more time as she had done when He was just a little boy running home with scraped knees. She wanted to wipe the blood that was crusting His eyes. She looked at His hands now cruelly nailed to wood and remembered how He had learned from His father how to use nails to hold together, not to tear apart; to create beauty, not to destroy it.

"Father, forgive them, for they do not know what they are doing" (Luke 23:34).

His voice was raspy and dry, but she heard every word. Even this cauldron of pain had not changed Him. They could nail His wrists to a tree, but they could not nail their bitterness into His heart, no matter what they did to Him.

He spoke again, this time to just one man, to one of those

being executed beside Him.

"I tell you the truth, today you will be with me in paradise" (v. 43).

That criminal had not begun the day in faith. He had mocked and cried out with the rest of them until he heard those first words: *Forgive them . . .*

Forgive them! That such a thing was still possible in this broken and barbaric place was stunning, impossible. She watched the man struggle and twist his body to look into her son's eyes, and the dying criminal saw what she already knew: *Behold, the Lamb of God, who takes away the sin of the world.*

In these last moments on earth, this wretched soul found freedom. Jesus spoke again, this time to her: "Dear woman, here is your son"!

Then to John, His dearest friend: "Here is your mother"! (John 19:26–27).

As Jesus turned His full attention on her, He looked deep into her soul. The love in that gaze was almost more painful to bear than watching His battered body struggle for air. How could one woman's heart contain this much pain without tearing apart? She felt John's arm wrap around her shoulders. He would take care of her now, and she would let him rest his head and sob on her breast.

Jesus spoke again: "I am thirsty" (John 19:28).

She watched as one of the soldiers dipped a sponge into the wine and held it to His lips. The pungent smell of the wine carried on the breeze reached Mary.

He spoke just once more, three words: "It is finished" (v. 30).

As He bowed his head, Mary knew that He was gone. But the way He bowed his head was so deliberate. It wasn't as someone beaten to death in body and spirit, but as One laying down His head after a long, long day, after completing an impossible task. It was a quiet declaration of victory.

THE LEAST OF THESE

A Jewess from the tribe of Judah, Mary was engaged to Joseph, a carpenter in Nazareth. Mary and Joseph came from poor families. We know that because after Jesus was born, they took to the temple the sacrificial gift of two turtledoves or pigeons, not a lamb (Leviticus 12:8). This was a provision made for the poorest of the poor. If you ever feel that you don't measure up to those around you, remember the kind of family in which God chose to place His Son.

And remember how the angel appeared to Mary. There is no account of anyone else being with her at the time. I think it would have been much easier for her if Gabriel had appeared when she was having dinner with her family. Then she would have had eyewitnesses to this unprecedented event. But that's not what happened. Mary would have to carry this sacred charge alone for some time: "You will be with child and give birth to a son" (Luke 1:31). What is amazing to me is that Mary didn't question how the pregnancy would impact her life, only how it would be possible since she was still a virgin. God is never grieved by our honest questions, just by our unbelief.

When Mary learns that she will conceive by the Holy Spirit, she utters these words: "I am the Lord's servant . . . May it be to me as you have said" (v. 38).

So here we have a poor, young teenager welcoming the will of God and knowing only some of what it will cost her. She will have to tell her parents and her fiancé: by law Joseph can publicly disgrace her, and she would never be able to find a husband. She could even be stoned to death. Mary first told Joseph, who was obviously devastated but didn't want to hurt Mary more than he had to, so he decided to divorce her quietly. God, in His mercy, sent an angel to Joseph to let him know that Mary was speaking the truth (Matthew 1:20–21).

THROUGH A MOTHER'S EYES

Later, what did Mary think about as she watched Jesus grow into a man? How many things might she have wondered about Him as she saw Him perform miracles and wonders at the beginning of His ministry? This tiny One she welcomed into their humble home had grown into a Man who was redefining what home is, who family is, and what our future can look like.

Jesus performed His first miracle at a friend's wedding, Mary saw Jesus take something ordinary—water—and make it exceptional—extra good wine. As she watched that day, she knew the journey to Calvary had begun. Wine at a wedding was a small thing, but then came the miracles of healing and of feeding massive crowds. His popularity grew and she knew the tide was turning: the Jewish religious leaders began to take a stand against Christ. When He was a little boy, she could use the four walls of her home to protect Him, but no more.

Did God see what was happening?

$\mathcal{D}$ID IT ALL GO WRONG?

As Mary watched Jesus hang in agony on the cross, did she understand that this was part of the plan, or did she believe that darkness had put out the light? Jesus' words to the thief on the cross offered him life beyond this life. But when? Where?

I wonder if Mary thought back to her response to Gabriel that day: "I am the Lord's servant," she had answered. "May it be to me as you have said" (Luke 1:38).

May it be to me as You have said.

What large words! Did Mary want to take them back? Don't you think she must have questioned God's plan and whether He was even in control? Haven't we all been there at times?

Standing at the foot of the cross and seeing a sign roughly nailed above Jesus' head—JESUS OF NAZARETH, KING OF THE JEWS—Mary may have thought back to the gifts brought by

THEY COULD *Nail* HIS WRISTS TO A TREE,

but they could not nail their bitterness into His hear

o matter what they did to him.

those noble men from the East. There had been gold and frank-incense—gifts fit for a king. The third gift, the myrrh, now made sense. Myrrh was an herb used to embalm the dead. As Mary watched her son's lifeless, bloodied body, did she wonder, *Is this it?*

THE PAIN OF DISAPPOINTMENT

I saved this promise—"I have gone to prepare a place for you"—until the last chapter for a couple of reasons. First and foremost, there are some things in this life that have no answer this side of eternity.

Ask any parent who has lost a child. You know pain and a depth of grief that no one else knows, and it is only when you are finally in the presence of Christ and reunited with that little one that the gaping wound will be healed and whole.

$\mathscr{A}$RE YOU THE ONE?

When, if ever, have you found yourself overwhelmed and practically immobilized by pain, yet because of your commitment to Christ, you take the next step and the next, confident that He is worth it? You and I live in the post-Crucifixion and post-Resurrection era, so even the darkest nights hold the promise of home for those of us who have placed our faith in Jesus. But what about those people who walked through nightmares *before* that Easter Sunday morning that changed everything?

And what if you had spent your life preparing the way for Christ, the Messiah, the One in whom every promise would be fulfilled, but when He arrived, everything about Him seemed wrong? No one could have prepared the way more completely or with more passion than John the Baptist, but when Christ, the Shelter of all God's promises, appeared, John was shaken to his core.

Few New Testament stories move me as deeply as the story of John the Baptist, especially the part about how he died. I'm referring not to the actual execution, which was a brutal, callous affair, but to what was happening inside John's heart and mind before he died.

A child of the wilderness and used to wide-open spaces, John had been confined to a dungeon. Having spent his whole life preparing for the moment when he would say, "Make straight the way for the Lord" (John 1:23), he now sat in a dank cell, his life apparently in Herod's hands, and still the promised kingdom had not come.

Where was the promised liberation? I can't imagine the disappointment and confusion and despair that must have settled on John. Jesus did not look like the Messiah to John. As doubts began to plague him, he wondered if he had gotten his life's work all wrong. What if he had prepared the way for Messiah but identified the wrong person? So he asked two of his disciples to find Jesus and ask Him this question: "Are you the one who was to come, or should we expect someone else?" (Luke 7:20).

And what must that question have done to Christ's heart? How He must have wanted to tell John the Baptist what was going to happen. He must have longed to liberate John from jail so that he could witness the Resurrection, but that was not God's plan. So Jesus sent a message back to John with a strange statement at the end. He told the messengers to tell John: "The blind receive sight, the lame walk, those who have leprosy are cured, the deaf hear, the dead are raised, and the good news is preached to the poor. Blessed is the man who does not fall away on account of me" (vv. 22–23).

In the first part of the statement, Jesus quoted from Isaiah 61, but He did not quote the last part of the text, "to proclaim freedom for the captives and release from darkness for the prisoners" (v. 1:1). There would be no liberation from prison for John. In essence Jesus said, *I'm not coming for you, John. Others will taste of the liberty that I bring, but not you, not today.* Instead, Jesus said, "Blessed is the man who does not fall away on account of me."

How would that message have impacted John? *You spent your whole life getting the stage set for Me. Now I am doing what Messiah is supposed to do, John, but not for you. And I have just one question for you, John: Do you still love Me?*

I can't read about this last brutal phase in John's life without weeping. He lived his whole life denying himself any sort of luxury or indulgence, and then he placed his head on a block with only the executioner at his side. John never saw what the road home through Christ was going to look like.

Christ's question for John the Baptist is a question that each one of us must answer at some point: Will you love and serve a God you do not always understand? And there are heartaches in life that will make no sense this side of eternity. As C. G. Moore writes, "I know of no hours more trying to faith than those in which Jesus multiplies evidences of his power and does not use it."[1]

OUR PROMISE, OUR HOPE, OUR HOME

Paul expressed this challenging reality so beautifully when he wrote, "Now we see but a poor reflection as in a mirror; then we shall see face to face. Now I know in part; then I shall know fully, even as I am fully known" (1 Corinthians 13:12).

So I ask you, with the deepest respect for the pain you have walked through, where is the dungeon in your life? Have you cried out to Jesus or sent Him messages asking Him to shine some light into your dark night? Perhaps, like John, you have seen Him do amazing things for other people, but no one has come to rescue you. Will you hear Him ask you as He asked John, *Do you still love Me? Will you tuck your life into the cleft of the Rock and let Me be your Shelter there? The wind will still howl and the night will still be dark, but I will never, ever leave you. That is My promise to you, and until you make it all the way home, I will be your home. I will be your Shelter.*

We are a people who do not live for this world. This is not our home. And until we finally see Jesus face-to-face, He has promised that He will never leave us. He has promised that He has gone ahead of us to prepare a place for us. What John could not see as he placed his head on the executioner's block was that the Shelter was almost complete.

THE SHELTER IS COMPLETE

Construction started one night when a young girl, far away from home, gave birth in a place that offered little of the kind of shelter a mother wants for her newborn baby. The canopy that night was heaven, and angels sang, "Glory to God in the highest and on earth peace to men on whom his favor rests" (Luke 2:14). As Christ grew into manhood and began His ministry, His life was a divine show-and-tell of the heart of God, but no one understood. No one saw what He was building because that is human nature: we see what we want to see and often miss the greatest gift of all.

Some people saw this Jesus of Nazareth as a warrior because they wanted revenge against those who had oppressed them for so long. Some saw Him only as a miracle worker because they wanted life to be fixed, to make sense, and they wanted it now. Some saw Him as a man who spoke the truth in a world of half truths but few recognized that He *is* the truth. With every act of love and kindness, every word of rebuke that cut through religious pretense, Jesus was laying the foundation for one radical statement that would change the world forever. When the final drop of His blood fell from the cross onto the dirt at its base and Jesus cried out, "It is finished," the Shelter was complete. Perhaps those who listened thought those words marked the end. How could they have known that those words marked the *beginning* of our liberty, our freedom? The Shelter is complete!

One day we will join John the Baptist and worship at the feet of Christ. You will be there, and so will I, along with every man, woman, and child who has put their trust and faith in Jesus Christ.

There are many things in this life I don't know, but I do know this: when we finally see Jesus, all of life's pain and suffering will be worth it.

There will be many mothers in the crowd, but I hope I catch a glimpse of Mary. We left her at the foot of the cross, but that's not where she stayed. No, she was, even at the end, looking for her Jesus.

I wonder who told Mary first that Jesus was alive.

Was it John? I imagine him running as fast as he could (and he makes a point in his gospel that he was faster than Peter!), throwing his arms around her fragile shoulders, and telling her, "Jesus is alive!"

As she wiped the tears from her cheek, she knew that she would see her son again, but this time He would be her Savior. This time He would be the one to wipe the tears from her eyes.

He is our hope.

And He is our home.

This is Christ's promise, given to help us keep our hearts set on being home with Him, with God the Father, with the Holy Spirit. Jesus has gone to prepare a place for us, but He left behind flagstones on which we can stand and a path for getting there. It is not simply that He has gone to prepare a place for us, but that His death and resurrection have made it possible for us to be there with Him forever. Christ will return and take us with Him to His home, our home. That is the glorious gift of the gospel.

And now, until you see Jesus face-to-face, may you find shelter in His glorious promises.

ENDNOTES

Chapter 4: Confidence / *God Is Either Sovereign or He's Not*

1. Edwin and Lillian Harvey and E. Hey, *They Knew Their God*, vol. 1 (Harvey and Tait Publishers, 1980; Old Tract Path Society, 1996), about Samuel Logan Brendle (1860–1936), "Soldier and Servant."

Chapter 6: Grace / *It's Not Too Good to Be True*

1. According to the Web site Marriage 101, the divorce rate in America for a first marriage is 41 percent; for a second marriage it is 60 percent ("Divorce Rates in America," http://marriage101.org/divorce-rates-in-america/).

Chapter 7: Hope / *God Said It; I Believe It*

1. Randy Elrod as quoted on his blog on June 15, 2010 (www.randyelrod.com), in a post titled "The Lie About Sexual Inequality."

2. Helen Roseveare, *Give Me This Mountain* (Gleanies House, Fearn, Ross-shire, Scotland: Christian Focus, 2006, 1966), 86.

3. Tonya Stoneman, "Can You Thank Me for This?" (online at www.suffering.net/thank.htm).

Chapter 9: More / *Why Am I Settling for Less?*

1. *The New Bible Dictionary* (Leicester, England: IVP, 1962), s.v. "blessed."

2. C. S. Lewis, *The Weight of Glory* (New York: HarperCollins, 2001), 26.

Chapter 10: Home / *The Shelter Is Complete*

1. C. G. Moore as quoted by W. H. Griffith Thomas, *Outline Studies in the Book of Luke* (Grand Rapids: Kregel, 1998), 129.

**If you have enjoyed this book
or it has touched your life in some way,
we would love to hear from you.**

Please send your comments to:
Hallmark Book Feedback
P.O. Box 419034
Mail Drop 215
Kansas City, Missouri 64141

Or e-mail us at:
booknotes@hallmark.com